Key Concepts
in
American History

Abolitionism

Key Concepts in American History

Key Concepts
in
American History

Abolitionism

Reyna Eisenstark

Jennifer L. Weber, Ph.D.
General Editor
University of Kansas

CHELSEA HOUSE
PUBLISHERS
An imprint of Infobase Publishing

Chelsea House
An imprint of Infobase Publishing
132 West 31st Street
New York NY 10001

Library of Congress Cataloging-in-Publication Data

Eisenstark, Reyna.
   Abolitionism / Reyna Eisenstark ; Jennifer L. Weber, general editor.
      p. cm. – (Key concepts in American history)
   Includes bibliographical references and index.
   ISBN 978-1-60413-220-5 (hardcover)
1. Antislavery movements—United States—Encyclopedias—Juvenile literature. 2. Abolitionists—United States—History—19th century—Encyclopedias—Juvenile literature. 3. Slaves—Emancipation—United States—Encyclopedias—Juvenile literature. 4. African Americans—History—To 1863—Encyclopedias—Juvenile literature. 5. African Americans—History—1863–1877—Encyclopedias—Juvenile literature. I. Weber, Jennifer L., 1962- II. Title.
   E449.E455 2009
   326′.80973—dc22

2009023374

Chelsea House books are available at special discounts when purchased in bulk quantities for businesses, associations, institutions, or sales promotions. Please call our Special Sales Department in New York at (212) 967-8800 or (800) 322-8755.

You can find Chelsea House on the World Wide Web at http://www.chelseahouse.com

Cover printed by Bang Printing, Brainerd, MN
Book printed and bound by Bang Printing, Brainerd, MN
Date printed: May 2010
Printed in the United States of America

10 9 8 7 6 5 4 3 2 1

This book is printed on acid-free paper and contains 30 percent postconsumer recycled content.

Acknowledgments
p. 1: Library of Congress, Prints and Photographs Division; pp. 17, 29, 39, 64, 68, 83, 95: The Granger Collection, New York; p. 54: Art Resource; p. 103: NY Jacket cover from *Uncle Tom's Cabin* by Harriet Beecher Stowe. Used by permission of Bantam Books, a division of Random House, Inc.

Contents

Viewpoints About Abolitionism

List of Illustrations

Photos

Maps

Reader's Guide
to Abolitionism

The list that follows is provided as an aid to readers in locating articles on the big topics or themes in American abolitionist history. The Reader's Guide arranges all of the A to Z entries in *Key Concepts in American History: Abolitionism* according to these **8 key concepts** of the social studies curriculum: **Abolitionists, Issues and Ideas; Laws and Legislation; Literature and Newspapers; People and Politics; Religion; Society and Groups;** and **Territories and Places.** Some articles appear in more than one category, helping readers see the links between topics.

Abolitionists
Adams, John Quincy
  (1767–1848)
Douglass, Frederick
  (1818–1895)
Garrett, Thomas (1789–1871)
Garrison, William Lloyd
  (1805–1879)
Quakers
Sumner, Charles (1811–1874)
Truth, Sojourner (1797–1883)
Tubman, Harriet
  (c. 1820–1913)

Issues and Ideas
Emancipation Proclamation
  (1863)
Gradualism
Immediatism
Popular Sovereignty
Racism
Slavery
U.S. Mail, Censorship of

Laws and Legislation
Compromise of 1850
Congress, United States
Dred Scott Decision (1857)
Emancipation Proclamation
  (1863)
Fugitive Slave Law (1850)

Kansas-Nebraska Act (1854)
Missouri Compromise (1820)
Sumner, Charles (1811–1874)
Thirteenth Amendment
  (1865)

Literature and Newspapers
Liberator, The (newspaper)
North Star, The
Slave Narratives
Slave's Friend, The
Uncle Tom's Cabin (1852)

People and Politics
Adams, John Quincy
  (1767–1848)
Clay, Henry (1777–1852)
Douglass, Frederick
  (1818–1895)
Garrett, Thomas (1789–1871)
Garrison, William Lloyd
  (1805–1879)
Lincoln-Douglas Debates
Popular Sovereignty
Quakers
Racism
Republican Party and
  Abolitionism
Sumner, Charles (1811–1874)
Taylor, Zachary (1784–1850)

Truth, Sojourner (1797–1883)
Tubman, Harriet
  (c. 1820–1913)
U.S. Mail, Censorship of
Webster, Daniel (1782–1852)

Religion
Bialystoker Synagogue
Quakers
Slavery

Society and Groups
American Anti-Slavery
  Society
American Convention of
  Abolition Societies
  (1794–1837)
Bialystoker Synagogue
Massachusetts Anti-Slavery
  Society
Quakers
Republican Party and
  Abolitionism
Slavery

Territories and Places
Bialystoker Synagogue
Canada and the Abolitionist
  Movement
Harpers Ferry
Underground Railroad

In 1619, the first Africans were brought to the **colony** of Virginia, in what would later become the United States. By the late 1600s, the growing need for labor, especially in the South, led to the institutionalization of slavery. At this same time, some American **colonists**, most notably the Quakers, called for the end, or abolition, of slavery.

After the **ratification** of the U.S. Constitution in 1788, most Northern states began to abolish slavery. Many northerners believed that slavery was opposed to the ideals of equality and self-government put forth in the Constitution. Others concluded that the keeping of slaves was not profitable in the North, which had a shorter growing season than did the South. Soon after ratification, the first abolitionist societies were organized. The invention of the cotton gin in 1793, however, increased the demand for slave labor on cotton **plantations**, and slavery became even more widespread throughout the South. Although abolitionist and antislavery sentiment grew during the early 1800s, slavery was finally abolished by the Thirteenth Amendment in 1865.

1775 Philadelphia Society for Promoting the Abolition of Slavery formed.

1788 The U.S. Constitution is ratified; protects slavery.

1789 Thomas Garrett, well-known abolitionist who later helped free more than 2,500 slaves, born in Delaware.

1793 First Fugitive Slave Law passed by Congress.

1794 American Convention of Abolition Societies formed.

1797 Sojourner Truth born enslaved in upstate New York.

1805 William Lloyd Garrison, founder of the abolitionist newspaper *The Liberator*, born in Massachusetts.

1816 American Colonization Society founded to encourage freed blacks to return to Africa.

1818 Frederick Douglass born enslaved in Easton, Maryland.

1820 Missouri Compromise passed by Congress; Harriet Tubman born enslaved in Bucktown, Maryland.

1821 Missouri admitted to the Union as a slave state.

1826 Willett Street Methodist Episcopal Church built; serves as stop on the Underground Railroad; later becomes Bialystoker Synagogue in New York City.

1831 Former U.S. president John Quincy Adams elected to the House of Representatives; William Lloyd Garrison first publishes *The Liberator.*

1832 Garrison founds Massachusetts Anti-Slavery Society.

1833 American Anti-Slavery Society founded in Philadelphia; slavery outlawed in Canada and all other British possessions.

1835 American Anti-Slavery Society begins mailing abolitionist materials to the South.

Abolitionism (1775–1865)

1836 "Gag rule," which prevents the discussion of petitions about slavery, passed in U.S. House of Representatives.

1838 Fredrick Douglass escapes from slavery.

1839 The African slaves aboard the *Amistad* revolt.

1841 *Amistad* case reaches U.S. Supreme Court; John Quincy Adams (1767–1848) successfully defends the Africans involved.

1844 "Gag rule" ends in U.S. House of Representatives.

1845 Frederick Douglass writes *Narrative of the Life of Frederick Douglass, an American Slave, Written by Himself.*

1846 Mexican-American War begins.

1847 Frederick Douglass publishes the *North Star,* an abolitionist newspaper.

1846 Mexican-American War ends.

1850 President Zachary Taylor (1849–1850) dies; Compromise of 1850, a series of five laws, passed by Congress; California admitted to the Union as a free state.

1852 *Uncle Tom's Cabin* published.

1854 Kansas-Nebraska Act passed; Republican Party founded.

1856 Abolitionist Senator Charles Sumner of Massachusetts is beaten unconscious on the Senate floor by South Carolina representative Brooks Preston; warfare breaks out in Kansas over slavery.

1857 *Dred Scott* decision holds that both free and enslaved African Americans are not citizens.

1858 Lincoln-Douglas debates confront issue of slavery; Douglas wins reelection to Illinois senate.

1859 John Brown unsuccessfully raids U.S. arsenal at Harpers Ferry.

1860 Abraham Lincoln (1809–1865) elected 16th president.

1861 Civil War begins; Kansas admitted to the Union as a free state.

1863 Lincoln issues the Emancipation Proclamation.

1865 Civil War ends; Lincoln assassinated; Thirteenth Amendment to the Constitution outlaws slavery.

1866 Susan B. Anthony, Lucretia Mott, Elizabeth Cady Stanton, and Frederick Douglass found the American Equal Rights Association.

1896 In *Plessy v. Ferguson,* the United States Supreme Court rules that "separate but equal" facilities for whites and African Americans are constitutional.

1954 United States Supreme Court issues its landmark decision in *Brown v. Board of Education,* ruling that separate facilities are "inherently unequal."

1964 Congress passes Civil Rights Act, which forbade discrimination based on race or sex.

1965 Congress passes the Voting Rights Act, knocking down the remaining barriers that prevented African Americans from voting.

2009 144 years after slavery is abolished in the United States, the American people inaugurate Barack Obama as their first African American president.

Preface

The United States was founded on ideas. Those who wrote the U.S. Constitution were influenced by ideas that began in Europe: reason over religion, human rights over the rights of kings, and self-governance over tyranny. Ideas, and the arguments over them, have continued to shape the nation. Of all the ideas that influenced the nation's founding and its growth, 10 are perhaps the most important and are singled out here in an original series—KEY CONCEPTS IN AMERICAN HISTORY. The volumes bring these concepts to life, *Abolitionism, Colonialism, Expansionism, Federalism, Industrialism, Internationalism, Isolationism, Nationalism, Progressivism*, and *Terrorism*.

These books examine the big ideas, major events, and influential individuals that have helped define American history. Each book features three sections. The first is an overview of the concept, its historical context, the debates over the concept, and how it changed the history and growth of the United States. The second is an encyclopedic, A-to-Z treatment of the people, events, issues, and organizations that help to define the "-ism" under review. Here, readers will find detailed facts and vivid histories, along with referrals to other books for more details about the topic.

Interspersed throughout the entries are many high-interest features: "History Speaks" provides excerpts of documents, speeches, and letters from some of the most influential figures in American history. "History Makers" provides brief biographies of key people who dramatically influenced the country. "Then and Now" helps readers connect issues of the nation's past with present-day concerns.

In the third part of each volume, "Viewpoints," readers will find longer primary documents illustrating ideas that reflect a certain point of view of the time. Also included are important government documents and key Supreme Court decisions.

The KEY CONCEPTS series also features "Milestones in. . . ," time lines that will enable readers to quickly sort out how one event led to another, a glossary, and a bibliography for further reading.

People make decisions that determine history, and Americans have generated and refined the ideas that have determined U.S. history. With an understanding of the most important concepts that have shaped our past, readers can gain a better idea of what has shaped our present.

Jennifer L. Weber, Ph.D.
Assistant Professor of History, University of Kansas
General Editor

What Is Abolitionism?

Any discussion about the history of the United States could not be complete without a discussion of the opposition to slavery. That's what abolitionism was—a long-standing movement that called for the end to the practice of slavery in the United States.

The former slaves of South Carolina plantation owner and Confederate general Thomas F. Drayton pose in this early photograph, taken in Hilton Head, South Carolina. The plantation's main manor house was burned during the Civil War, possibly by Union troops but more probably by the newly freed slaves.

Abolitionism began as a moral issue, later turned into a political issue, and ultimately led to a war that threatened to split apart the country. The victory of the Union in the Civil War (1861–1865) kept the United States as one nation and returned the **seceding** Southern states to the Union.

THE BEGINNINGS OF AMERICAN SLAVERY

The practice of slavery in the United States began when the 13 American **colonies** were a part of the British Empire. However, slavery as an institution has existed in some form throughout human history. A slave was generally understood throughout history to be someone owned as "property" by someone else, usually with no rights or freedoms. Yet, in the ancient world, slavery was not always a permanent condition. In many societies, slaves could become citizens after a period of time. In addition, slaves were not considered the lowest class of people. Many worked as farmers and household servants, but some owned property and were wealthy. Moreover, once slaves were freed, they were rarely identified with their previous status as slaves. For many families, owning slaves merely symbolized wealth and power and was not a necessary source of labor. Finally, for much of human history, slavery was not an inherited condition as it was in the Americas.

The African slave trade By the fifteenth century, however, a new kind of slavery was introduced to the world. The African slave trade developed as part of a system of international commerce between Europe, Africa, and North and South America. European traders exported manufactured goods to the west coast of Africa, where they would be exchanged for slaves. Millions of slaves were in turn sold in the Americas, though the majority went to Brazil.

Most slaves who were sold to Europeans through the Atlantic slave trade either had been captured in local wars or were enslaved as punishment for certain crimes or as repayment of a debt. As a result of the European demand for slaves in the sixteenth century, increasing numbers of Africans were enslaved by rival groups or for minor crimes. Professional slave traders from various European countries, including England, France, Holland, Spain, and Portugal, set up slave-trading posts on the coast of West Africa.

Once Africans were captured from their villages to be sold as slaves, they were bound together and marched to the Atlantic coast, sometimes for hundreds of miles. As many as half of the people who were forced to march died on the way. Once they were sold, slaves were chained together and forced onto ships. The journey to the Americas became known as the Middle Passage; slave ships traveled from Europe to Africa, then to the Americas, and back to Europe again.

First Africans in the Thirteen Colonies Before the late 1600s, the number of slaves who reached what is now the United States was very small because the institution of slavery grew slowly. In the early 1600s, American **colonists** mostly used **indentured servants** for labor. Some Africans were also employed as indentured servants and were allowed freedom after their period of service had ended. However, as English settlers faced a shortage of white indentured servants in the late 1600s, they began to import thousands of slaves directly from Africa.

Slavery was a racially based institution that would last in the United States until 1865. By the early 1700s, it had become clear that Africans—not Indians—would be enslaved. Beginning in 1705, new laws, called "slave codes," clearly defined the status of Africans as slaves only.

Furthermore, by the early 1800s, slavery was closely tied to the economy of the South, which differed greatly from the economy of the North. Although most Northerners were farmers, manufacturing had become an important part of the economy by midcentury. Northern cities had grown large because of the growth of factories and the need for factory workers. Most Americans in the South also were farmers. The majority owned small farms and could not afford slaves. However, a number of wealthy farmers grew valuable cash crops, such as cotton, on huge plantations. These planters produced most of the South's wealth and depended upon slave labor for their economic survival.

The striking differences in Northern and Southern economies led to very different attitudes toward the practice of slavery. Southerners began to see slavery as an economic necessity, whereas many Northerners began to question its morality. During the American Revolution (1775–1783), a fight for freedom and independence, many people in the North freed their slaves. Thousands of other slaves escaped to freedom. By the early 1800s, every Northern state had abolished slavery either by court decisions or by a plan of gradual emancipation. In the South, however, slavery continued to grow as the economic need for it increased. Rather than invest in farm equipment or land, as people in the North did, Southerners put most of their money into buying more slaves. Slavery was by then considered a normal part of Southern life.

BEGINNINGS OF THE ABOLITIONIST MOVEMENT

At the same time, the **abolitionist** movement, whose followers demanded the end of slavery in the United States, began to grow. In the late 1600s, the Religious Society of Friends, or Quakers, became the first group to organize an opposition to slavery. Soon the movement began to expand. Early American abolitionist groups adopted the concept of gradualism, believing slavery should be phased out slowly so that the economy of the South would not be disrupted. Some white abolitionists also believed that, over time, American slavery would die out on its own.

The early antislavery movement Many early opponents of slavery also supported colonization, which involved freeing all slaves and then sending them to a colony in Africa. Those abolitionists who felt that free blacks could not easily enter American society saw this migration as a good solution to the problem of slavery. By the late 1820s, however, it became obvious that colonization was impractical. Very few African Americans wanted to move to Africa. Many also recognized colonization as a way for the United States to simply remove its black population.

By the 1830s, the American abolitionist movement had changed its focus, mostly because of the leadership of editor and publisher William Lloyd Garrison (1805–1879), who demanded immediatism, or the immediate freeing of slaves and equal rights for African Americans. Garrison helped found the American Anti-Slavery Society in 1833, and following his lead, hundreds of antislavery societies were created in the North. Antislavery societies spread their message by mailing pamphlets and newspapers denouncing slavery and by sending antislavery **petitions** to the U.S. Congress. They also sent lecturers around the country to deliver antislavery speeches, and they published slave narratives—firsthand accounts of the lives of African Americans who had escaped from slavery.

An important part of the antislavery movement was a network that became known as the Underground Railroad. The Underground Railroad was a system of safe houses and hiding places that used "conductors" to help runaway slaves escape to freedom. Though many people, white and African American, participated in the Underground Railroad, it was not run by any single organization. Slaves traveled along the Railroad, escaping from slaveholding states in the South to free states in the North or to Canada.

A few years after the start of the new antislavery movement of the 1830s, the movement had divided over various issues. William Lloyd Garrison took a more radical view, demanding equal rights for women, rejecting the U.S. Constitution as a proslavery document, and calling for the breakup of the Union into free states and slave states. Garrison also felt that slavery was a moral issue and not a political one. However, other abolitionist leaders, including free African American Frederick Douglass (1818–1895), turned to politics as a way to end slavery. With abolitionism as their main platform, two new, but short-lived, political parties formed in the United States: the Liberty Party in 1840 and the Free-Soil Party in 1848. Then in 1854, the Republican Party was founded. It sought to prevent slavery from expanding into the newly acquired western territories.

THE SLAVERY DEBATE IN AMERICAN GOVERNMENT

During this time, the U.S. Congress also debated the question of slavery and its impact upon the growing nation. As more territories applied for statehood in the mid-1800s, the question of whether they should allow slavery was answered by a series of compromises that never really resolved the issue.

Compromises In 1820, the passage of the Missouri Compromise kept the balance between slave and free states by admitting Missouri as a slave state and Maine as a free state. In addition, Congress determined that any new states north of Missouri's southern border would be free states, and states south of that border would be slave states.

After the Mexican-American War (1846–1848), the United States acquired 525,000 square miles (1.36 million square km) of land from Mexico. Once again, Congress resorted to compromise over the issue of whether to allow slavery into the new territories. Among other provisions, the Compromise of 1850 admitted California as a free state and allowed the settlers of New Mexico to decide whether or not to allow slavery in the territory, a concept known as popular sovereignty. This compromise also strengthened the Fugitive Slave Law, which made it illegal to help runaway slaves or prevent their arrest, as well as made it much easier for Southern **slaveholders** to go into free states and claim their "property."

The Kansas-Nebraska Act Just four years after the Compromise of 1850, Congress passed the Kansas-Nebraska Act, which established that the territories of Kansas and Nebraska could decide for themselves whether or not to allow slavery. Violence in Kansas soon broke out between antislavery and proslavery settlers. As violence flared, Americans on both sides of the slavery question were becoming increasingly entrenched in their view and suspicious of the other side. Ultimately, compromise became impossible.

By the late 1850s, the antislavery movement had reached its peak as an increasing number of Northerners began to oppose slavery outright. Many believed the South planned to extend slavery across the entire United States and some Northerners wanted the federal government to step in. During the 1860 presidential election, former Illinois congressman Abraham Lincoln (1861–1865) ran as the candidate of the Republican Party. Believing that his election would mean the end of slavery in the United States, many white Southerners threatened to **secede** from the Union if Lincoln were elected. In December 1860, six weeks after Lincoln won the presidential race, South Carolina became the first Southern state to secede. A few months later, in April 1861, the Civil War (1861–1865) began.

Lincoln's Emancipation Proclamation of 1863, which declared the end of slavery in all areas not under Union control, was the beginning of the end of American slavery. The Thirteenth Amendment to the Constitution, ratified in 1865, finally made slavery illegal throughout the entire United States. The abolitionist movement had triumphed once and for all.

THE LEGACY OF THE ABOLITIONIST MOVEMENT

As a nation, the United States had split over the issue of slavery. Southerners defended their right to own slaves and considered slavery a local issue and not one to be decided by the federal government. Yet the North feared that, if the federal government did not control the spread of slavery, the institution would continue to grow throughout the country. As the American abolitionist movement grew stronger in its fight against slavery, the United States became even more divided.

With the start of the Civil War, the conflict between North and South became a long and brutal fight. More than 600,000 Union and Confederate soldiers lost their lives during the war. After Lincoln issued the Emancipation Proclamation, however, Northern war aims changed: Now the war was not only to save the Union but also to end slavery.

Although the Union victory in 1865 maintained the unity of the United States, it would take a long time to rebuild the country and solve the economic problems of the South. Now that all African Americans were freed, their rights and citizenship needed to be decided as well. As the country began the long process of Reconstruction, or rebuilding, its future was unclear. Yet one thing was certain: The institution of slavery would never exist within the United States again.

Still, racism continued to plague the nation. African Americans, though no longer enslaved, were deprived of the basic civil rights that white Americans took for granted. Many states, especially in the South, passed laws that provided for separate facilities, such as schools, hotels, theaters, and even drinking fountains, for African Americans and whites. The United States Supreme Court held, in the case of *Plessy v. Ferguson* (1896), that such laws were constitutional as long as the facilities were essentially equal. Clearly, however, facilities for African Americans were not equal to those of whites.

"Separate but equal" facilities existed throughout most of the nation until 1954. In that year, the Supreme Court ruled in the case of *Brown v. Board of Education of Topeka, Kansas,* that separate schools for white and African American children were "inherently unequal." The case is often cited as the beginning of the civil rights movement.

Throughout the next several decades, other barriers to racial segregation fell. In 1965, Congress passed the Voting Rights Act. This landmark legislation ensured that African Americans and other minorities could not be prevented from voting in local, state, and national elections. In the last decades of the twentieth century, the number of African American and other minority-elected officials increased significantly. By the early 2000s, African Americans were represented throughout the nation in every branch of government. Finally, in 2008, Americans elected Barack Obama (2009–) as the nation's first African American president. During his campaign for the presidency, Obama addressed the issue of race:

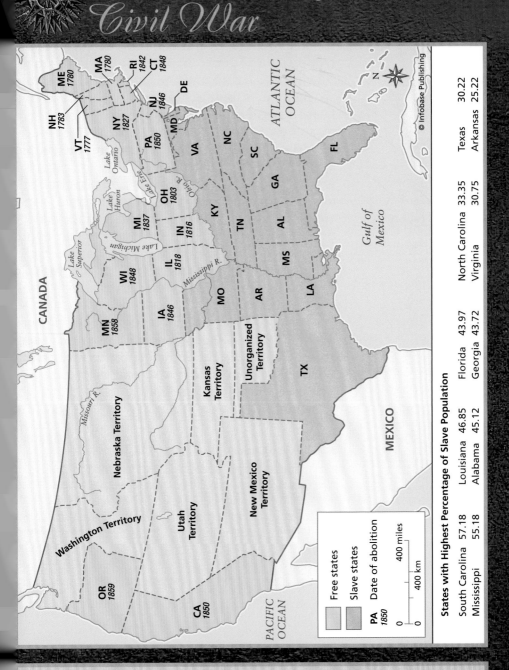

© Infobase Publishing

States with Highest Percentage of Slave Population

| South Carolina | 57.18 | Louisiana | 46.85 | Florida | 43.97 | North Carolina | 33.35 | Texas | 30.22 |
| Mississippi | 55.18 | Alabama | 45.12 | Georgia | 43.72 | Virginia | 30.75 | Arkansas | 25.22 |

The Northern states had begun abolishing slavery shortly after the American Revolution (1775–1783). Yet in the South, the enslaved population grew, especially after the invention of the cotton gin in 1793. By the outbreak of the Civil War (1861–1865), more than 50 percent of the population of South Carolina and Mississippi were enslaved blacks.

I am the son of a black man from Kenya and a white woman from Kansas. I was raised with the help of a white grandfather who survived a Depression to serve in Patton's Army during World War II and a white grandmother who worked on a bomber assembly line at Fort Leavenworth while he was overseas. I've gone to some of the best schools in America and lived in one of the world's poorest nations. I am married to a black American who carries within her the blood of slaves and slave owners—an inheritance we pass on to our two precious daughters. I have brothers, sisters, nieces, nephews, uncles and cousins, of every race and every hue, scattered across three continents, and for as long as I live, I will never forget that in no other country on Earth is my story even possible.

It's a story that hasn't made me the most conventional candidate. But it is a story that has seared into my genetic makeup the idea that this nation is more than the sum of its parts—that out of many, we are truly one.

FURTHER READING

McNeese, Tim. *The Abolitionist Movement: Ending Slavery.* New York: Chelsea House, 2007.

Stewart, James Brewer. *Abolitionist Politics and the Coming of the Civil War.* Amherst: University of Massachusetts Press, 2008.

Tackach, James. *American Social Movements—The Abolitionist Movement.* Farmington Hills, Mich.: Greenhaven Press, 2005.

Abolitionism
from
A–Z

A–B

Adams, John Quincy (1767–1848)

Sixth president of the United States (1825–1829), secretary of state, U.S. congressman from Massachusetts, and a fervent **abolitionist**. John Quincy Adams was the son of John Adams (1797–1801), the second president of the United States. Although John Quincy Adams served as president, it is his nine consecutive terms in the House of Representatives, from 1830 to 1848, for which he is best known for his support of putting an end to slavery.

John Quincy Adams entered politics in 1803 when he was elected to serve as a U.S. senator from Massachusetts. He later served as secretary of state under President James Monroe (1817–1825). Adams only served one term as president, losing to Andrew Jackson (1829–1837) in the 1828 election. After his defeat, Adams retired briefly but then decided to reenter politics; he became a U.S. representative from Massachusetts in 1831. He held this seat until his death, 17 years later.

As a congressman, John Quincy Adams became known as an outspoken opponent of slavery. Prior to this, he was not known as an abolitionist and, on certain occasions, supported the rights of **slaveholders.** However, his views began to change in his later years, and in Congress, he took an antislavery position. In 1831, the year that Adams joined the House of Representatives, abolitionist leader William Lloyd Garrison began publishing the abolitionist newspaper *The Liberator.* Many abolitionist groups sent **petitions** to Congress calling for the end of slavery. These petitions angered the members of Congress who supported slavery. In 1836, Congressman Henry Pinckney of South Carolina presented the first of what would become known as **gag rules.** It stated that any petitions received by Congress that related to slavery would not be read or discussed.

John Quincy Adams believed that the gag rules were a violation of the First Amendment's protection of freedom to petition. He felt that no matter what a person's position on slavery was, to refuse to read the petitions was unconstitutional. The gag rule remained in effect for nine years, from 1836 to 1844. Each year, the gag rule had to be renewed, and each year, Adams fought against it. Because of his powerful speeches before Congress, Adams was called "Old Man Eloquent."

During the years in which the gag rule was in effect, Adams was accused of treason and even received death threats. Adams continued to present petitions for the abolition of slavery and the slave trade to Congress, which congressmen would ultimately refuse to discuss. In October of 1837, Adams wrote in his diary, "I have gone as far upon this article, the abolition of slavery, as the public opinion of the free portion of the Union will bear, and so far that scarcely a slaveholding member of the House dares to vote with me upon any question."

Gradually, as antislavery sentiment in the North grew, more Northern members of Congress began to support Adams's argument against the gag rule. No matter what a person's opinion of slavery was, they believed, suppressing the right to petition was unconstitutional. In 1844, the gag rule was up for renewal again. This time, a majority of Congress voted with Adams, and the gag rule was finally lifted.

In 1841, John Quincy Adams argued successfully before the U.S. Supreme Court to win freedom for 53 Africans who had been captured and confined on the Spanish ship *Amistad.* For two days, he successfully argued the case on behalf of the Africans. Adams's argument was dramatic and convincing. The court ruled that the Africans were free because international slave trade was illegal under U.S. law. The Africans were allowed to return to Africa.

On February 21, 1848, John Quincy Adams was preparing to address the House of Representatives when he collapsed. He was carried to the Speaker's Room in the Capitol, where he died two days later.

See also: Amistad; Congress, United States.

FURTHER READING
Remini, Robert V. *John Quincy Adams.* New York: Times Books, 2002.
Wheelan, Joseph. *Mr. Adams's Last Crusade: John Quincy Adams's Extraordinary Post-Presidential Life in Congress.* New York: PublicAffairs Books, 2008.

American Anti-Slavery Society

Abolitionist group, founded in 1833, in Philadelphia, which called for an immediate end to slavery in the United States. Among the group's founders were abolitionists Theodore Weld, Arthur Tappan, Lewis Tappan, and William Lloyd Garrison. Garrison led the society until 1865, when slavery was officially abolished by the Thirteenth Amendment to the U.S. Constitution. The free African American Frederick Douglass was another leader of the society and often spoke at its meetings.

EARLY YEARS

By 1838, the society had more than 1,300 local chapters, with a membership of about 250,000. The society provided local antislavery groups with a national platform on which members could voice their concerns. The society sent speakers across the North to convince people of slavery's brutality. Unlike some other abolitionist groups, the American Anti-Slavery Society called for the immediate **emancipation** of all slaves. It also called for African Americans to receive the same political rights as whites, including the right to vote and to choose a job.

The society sent hundreds of **petitions** to the U.S. Congress calling for the end of slavery. Instead of addressing the slavery issue, however, in 1836 Congress imposed the **gag rule** at the insistence of the Southern, slaveholding states. The gag rule stated that Congress would not accept any petitions that pertained to slavery. One of the most outspoken opponents of the gag rule was Representative John Quincy Adams, who had earlier served as the sixth president of the United States (1825–1829). While in Congress, the former president worked to eliminate the gag rule, which was finally repealed in 1844.

In 1839, the society split into two groups because of differences in opinion. Many members did not fully support the society's leader, William Lloyd Garrison. Garrison was not only a vocal opponent of slavery but also a supporter of full equality for women.

From the Constitution of the American Anti-Slavery Society

The American Anti-Slavery Society was one of the best-known abolitionist groups in the years before the Civil War (1861–1865). Its constitution, written in December 1833, called for an immediate end to slavery throughout the United States. It also identified slavery as contrary to the ideals set forth in the Declaration of Independence.

Whereas the Most High God "hath made of one blood all nations of men to dwell on all the face of the earth," and hath commanded them to love their neighbors as themselves; and whereas, our National Existence is based upon this principle, as recognized in the Declaration of Independence, "that all mankind are created equal, and that they are endowed by their Creator with certain inalienable rights, among which are life, liberty, and the pursuit of happiness"; and whereas, after the lapse of nearly sixty years, since the faith and honor of the American people were pledged to this avowal, before Almighty God and the World, nearly one-sixth part of the nation are held in bondage by their fellow-citizens; and whereas, Slavery is contrary to the principles of natural justice, of our republican form of government, and of the Christian religion, and is destructive of the prosperity of the country, . . .

For example, he called for women to become more active in the abolitionist movement, a position with which many members disagreed. Further, he criticized the U.S. Constitution because it allowed slavery. He called for the nation to set up a new government that prohibited slavery, and he suggested that, if the South did not give up its slaves, the North should **secede** from the Union and form a separate country.

THE SOCIETY SPLITS IN TWO

Many members of the society thought that Garrison's ideas were too radical. They believed slavery was wrong, but they also felt that the U.S. Constitution had set up a lawful government that needed to be obeyed. This group of abolitionists hoped to elect government leaders who supported their view and who would peacefully change the laws to free the slaves. In 1840, many of these abolitionists joined the Liberty Party, a political party that opposed slavery. After losing two presidential elections, the Liberty Party joined with other abolitionist groups and formed the Free-Soil Party in 1848. Later, in 1854, most Free-Soilers joined the Republican Party.

Groups such as the American Anti-Slavery Society were instrumental in influencing government leaders to abolish slavery officially in 1865. In 1870, after the Civil War (1861–1865) and emancipation, its work done, the Society disbanded.

See also: Douglass, Frederick; Garrison, William Lloyd; Immediatism; Republican Party and Abolitionism; Thirteenth Amendment.

FURTHER READING

Fauchald, Nick. *William Lloyd Garrison: Abolitionist and Journalist.* Mankato, Minn.: Compass Point Books, 2005.

Lowence, Mason, ed. *Against Slavery: An Abolitionist Reader.* New York: Penguin Classics, 2000.

Miller, William Lee. *Arguing About Slavery: John Quincy Adams and the Great Battle in the United States Congress.* New York: Vintage, 1998.

American Convention of Abolition Societies (1794–1837)

Group formed in Philadelphia on January 1, 1794, by **delegates** from abolition societies in Connecticut, New York, New Jersey, Pennsylvania, Delaware, and Maryland. These societies joined together to become more effective in fighting for the abolishment of slavery on a national level.

In 1775, the Pennsylvania Society for Promoting the Abolition of Slavery became the first American **abolitionist** group. By 1793, there were abolitionist groups in New York, Rhode Island, Connecticut, and New Jersey. Smaller abolitionist societies were also formed in the Southern states of Delaware, Maryland, and Virginia. These early abolitionist societies focused on local issues of slavery, such as providing legal assistance to African Americans and protecting state abolition laws. Their work also involved national issues, however, and because of this, a number of groups felt it would be more effective to combine efforts.

On January 1, 1794, delegates from nine different Northern abolitionist societies organized the American Convention of Abolition Societies in Philadelphia. The object of the convention was "to increase the zeal and efficiency of the individual societies by its advice and encouragement" and "to take upon itself the chief responsibility in regard to national affairs." The convention voted to **petition** Congress to prohibit the slave trade and to appeal to the various state legislatures to abolish slavery. The different branches of the convention were expected to report on the number of free blacks in each state and on their property, employment, and well-being. The convention planned to meet every January until slavery was abolished nationally.

Once the American Convention of Abolition Societies was formed, it became the source of nearly all **petitions** sent to Congress regarding slavery. Though the convention's main goal was to bring about the end of slavery, in general members felt that it would be best achieved gradually, without causing too much disruption in the lives of **slaveholders** and African Americans. Much of the convention's work with freed blacks focused on education, which members believed was the key to African American success in American society. Each year, the American Convention sent out reports on the conditions of free blacks in the various states.

By the 1820s, the American Convention focused much of its effort on ending slavery and the slave trade in Washington, D.C. Abolitionists believed that allowing slavery to be practiced in the nation's capital sent a terrible image of the United States to the rest of the world. The American Convention sent numerous petitions regarding this issue to Congress until 1836, when Congress instituted the **gag rule** and would no longer accept any petitions that pertained to slavery.

The American Convention of Abolition Societies met every year, and sometimes twice a year, until 1837. Because of the gag rule in 1836, they could no longer petition Congress as a means to accomplish their goals. At the same time, groups such as the American Anti-Slavery Society became leaders of the abolitionist movement. The focus of the new groups was immediatism, or an immediate end to slavery and the immediate establishment of equality for African Americans.

See also: American Anti-Slavery Society; Congress, United States; Gradualism; Immediatism.

Amistad

Nineteenth-century Spanish schooner that was the site of an African slave revolt. The story of the *Amistad* begins in April 1839 when about 500 Africans were captured as slaves in West Africa. The Africans were then transported to Havana, Cuba, and sold at a slave market. Although slavery was legal in many countries at the time, the international slave trade had been banned by various countries, including Great Britain, Spain, and the United States. Despite this ban, an illegal slave trade continued and flourished. Fifty-three of the captured Africans were sold to two Cuban traders named Jose Ruiz and Pedro Montes. Ruiz and Montes planned to sell the Africans to a sugar plantation on the other side of the island. They brought the Africans onto the *Amistad* and set sail for the plantation.

THE REVOLT

Two days later, however, on July 1, 1839, several of the African captives freed themselves and took over the ship. They were led by a man named Sengbe, who later became known by the Spanish name Cinque. The African rebels killed the captain and the cook of the *Amistad*, leaving only Ruiz and Montes. The slave traders were spared but were ordered to sail the ship back to Africa. Ruiz and Montes tricked the Africans by steering east to Africa by day but turning the ship toward the United States by night. In August, the *Amistad* was forced to dock off the coast of Long Island, New York, after its supplies were nearly gone. The ship was soon discovered, on August 26, by the U.S. Coastal Survey. The *Amistad* was then towed to New London, Connecticut.

Montes and Ruiz claimed that the Africans on board the *Amistad* were slaves from Cuba who had murdered the captain and taken over the ship. The Africans were arrested, and a U.S. district judge ordered that they be tried in court on charges of murder, **mutiny,** and **piracy.** The Africans, who did not speak English or Spanish, were unable to defend themselves.

The Spanish ambassador soon became involved in the case and demanded that President Martin Van Buren (1837–1841) return the ship and the Africans to Ruiz and Montes.

Spain insisted that the Africans should be tried under Spanish law because they were Cuban slaves and Cuba was a Spanish colony. Van Buren was willing to do so, but by then the case had already gone to court.

THE FIRST TRIAL

By now, the story of the African slave revolt on the *Amistad* had caught the attention of American **abolitionists**. Lewis Tappan, a New York merchant and abolitionist, was contacted by Connecticut abolitionists soon after the *Amistad* arrived in its port. Tappan helped raise money for the legal defense of the Africans. Eventually, the abolitionists found a translator who could speak to the African captives. The Africans were finally able to dispute Ruiz's and Montes's claims. They explained that they were not slaves born in Cuba but instead had been kidnapped from Africa and had only been in Cuba for a few days. Their testimony helped establish the defense for the trial. In addition, Tappan had discovered that the documents Ruiz and Montes had presented, falsely showing that the Africans were slaves from Cuba, had been forged.

On January 7, 1840, the trial began in the District Court in Hartford, Connecticut. The judge, after reviewing the Africans' testimony and the forged documents, concluded that the Africans were free, even under Spanish law, because they had been illegally captured and sold in a slave market. The judge ordered that the African captives be returned to Africa.

This outraged President Martin Van Buren, who was worried that by doing so he would lose the support of Southern **slaveholders.** He ordered that the case be appealed to the Supreme Court. Tappan felt that the Africans needed a stronger defense team to help them win the case. He asked former president John Quincy Adams (1825–1829), who was now serving in Congress, to join the legal team. Adams was a powerful orator and was known to be in favor of abolition. For years, Adams had fought in Congress against the **gag rule**, which stated that any petitions received by Congress related to slavery would not be read or discussed. Adams was reluctant to take on the *Amistad* case, fearing he might lose, but he eventually agreed. As Adams wrote in his diary, "... what can I do for the cause of God and man, for the progress of human emancipation, for the suppression of the African slave-trade? Yet my conscience presses me on. . . ."

Joseph Cinque is shown in this portrait by Connecticut abolitionist and painter Nathaniel Jocelyn. Cinque was the leader of a group of Africans who, in 1839, overthrew the crew of the slave ship *Amistad*. They were eventually captured and jailed. After a trial that reached the U.S. Supreme Court, they were freed and made their way back to Africa.

THE SUPREME COURT DECISION

The *Amistad* case went before the Supreme Court on February 22, 1841. Adams's closing argument extended over two days and lasted eight-and-a-half hours in total. Adams argued that the Africans had been illegally enslaved, even by Spain's own laws. He also questioned the use of the term *property* to describe enslaved people. Adams pointed out that if the American president could hand these free men over to a foreign government, no one in the United States could ever be sure that they were truly free.

On March 9, 1841, Justice Joseph Story delivered the majority decision of the Supreme Court in the case of the *United States v. The Amistad.* Because the ownership papers from Ruiz and Montes were proven **forgeries,** the justices concluded that the captives had been kidnapped and their rebellion on the *Amistad* was in self-defense. Later, Story described

History Speaks

From John Quincy Adams's Arguments Before the Supreme Court in the Amistad Case

The case of the *Amistad* went before the Supreme Court on February 22, 1841. Adams argued before the Court that the African men on board had been illegally enslaved. The Supreme Court ruled in their favor, and by December, the men were returned to Africa.

This honorable Court will observe from the record that there were fifty-four Africans who left the Havana. Ruiz says in his libel that nine had died before they reached our shores. The marshal's return shows that they were dying day after day from the effects of their sufferings.... Although placed in a condition which, if applied to forty citizens of the United States, we should call cruel, shut up eighteen months in a prison, and enjoying only the tenderness which our laws provide for the worst of criminals, so great is the improvement of their condition from what it was in the hands of Ruiz, that they have perfectly recovered their health, and not one has died; when, before that time, they were perishing from hour to hour....

Who, then, are the tyrants and oppressors against whom our laws are invoked? Who are the innocent sufferers, for whom we are called upon to protect this ship against enemies and robbers? Certainly not Ruiz and Montes....

I said, when I began this plea, that my final reliance for success in this case was on this Court as a court of JUSTICE; and in the confidence this fact inspired that, in the administration of justice, in a case of no less importance than the liberty and the life of a large number of persons, this Court would not decide but on a due consideration of all the rights, both natural and social, of every one of these individuals. I have endeavored to show that they are entitled to their liberty from this Court....

Adams's argument as "extraordinary for its power and its bitter sarcasm, and its dealing with topics far beyond the record and point of discussion." In January 1842, the surviving 35 Africans from the *Amistad* returned to Africa.

Abolitionists viewed the Supreme Court's decision as a victory. They printed thousands of copies of the defense argument, hoping to convince even more Americans of the evils of slavery and the slave trade. However, the Court's decision did not address either the status of runaway slaves or the larger question of slavery in the United States. This question would return repeatedly until the country divided itself over the issue during the Civil War (1861–1865).

See also: Adams, John Quincy; Slavery.

Bialystoker Synagogue

Orthodox Jewish house of worship on the Lower East Side of New York City. During the early 1800s, a hidden room in the building was a stop for fugitive slaves on the Underground Railroad.

The **synagogue** was constructed originally in 1826 as the Willett Street Methodist Episcopal Church. In 1905, a **congregation** of Jews from Bialystok, Poland, bought the building, after which it became Bialystoker Synagogue. The building, which was constructed from local stone, became a New York City landmark in 1966. Much of its original details have been preserved, including a secret passageway. In a corner of what is now the separate women's gallery, there is a small hidden door in the wall. Behind this door is a wooden ladder that leads to an attic. Inside the attic, there are two small windows that dimly light the room. It was here that runaway slaves were hidden from the authorities until they could make their way to freedom.

Although slavery was abolished in the state of New York in 1827, the Fugitive Slave Law of 1850 made it ille-

gal to help runaway slaves. Therefore, New York City was not usually a destination for runaway slaves, though many still stopped there on their way to Canada. Canada was the ultimate destination for many slaves because slavery was illegal there and because, once in Canada, former slaves could not be legally returned to the United States.

Because Manhattan is surrounded by water, slaves often arrived there by boat. A number of known Underground Railroad stops in New York City were near water, including the Bialystoker Synagogue, which is close to the East River. From New York City, enslaved people could travel along the Hudson River to the Northern cities of Albany and Troy and then travel farther north to Canada.

Many safe places for slaves in New York City were in neighborhoods that had communities of free blacks, but they also included homes of Quakers, white **abolitionists**, and others willing to help slaves on their way to freedom. Because the punishment for helping runaway slaves was severe, there are few records of the secret passageways and safe houses associated with hiding escaped slaves. Slaves and the people who hid them often left only codes about hiding places, such as certain words that referred to specific locations. It was important for the preservation of the Underground Railroad not to leave any written records that might be discovered. This means that many stops along the Underground Railroad are only speculative, and many stops have yet to be uncovered. The Bialystoker Synagogue is an example of a known stop on the Underground Railroad that is still preserved today.

See also: Fugitive Slave Law; Underground Railroad.

Bleeding Kansas

See Kansas-Nebraska Act (1854); Popular Sovereignty.

Brooks, Preston

See Sumner, Charles.

Brown, John

See Harpers Ferry; Kansas-Nebraska Act (1854).

C

Canada and the Abolitionist Movement

Former British possession located to the north of the United States and its role in the American antislavery movement. After slavery was ended, or abolished, in Canada in 1833, a number of Canadian abolition societies formed to support the end of slavery in the United States. Canada was also a final destination for thousands of fugitive slaves traveling on the Underground Railroad, a secret network of hiding places that helped escaped slaves reach freedom.

THE END OF SLAVERY
IN CANADA

By the time that slavery was legally abolished in Canada, most slaves there had already gained their freedom. In 1793, John Graves Simcoe (1752–1806), the lieutenant governor of Canada, introduced an act to eliminate slavery gradually, which the Canadian legislature passed. It became illegal to bring new slaves into the colony, and children born to slaves would become free at age 25. In 1833, the **British Parliament** passed the Abolition Act, which declared that ". . . slavery shall be and is hereby utterly and forever abolished and declared unlawful throughout the British colonies, plantations, and possessions abroad."

The end of slavery in Canada greatly affected slaves in the United States. In 1793, the same year that slavery began to be phased out in Canada, the U.S. Congress passed its first Fugitive Slave Law. This law made it illegal for American citizens to help runaway slaves or prevent their arrest. As a result, Northern states were no longer safe destinations for escaping slaves, and many fugitives traveled farther north to Canada. In 1819, the U.S. government asked Canada to help return escaping slaves and asked if **slaveholders** could travel to Canada to reclaim their escaped slaves. However, Canada refused. Therefore, any American slave who reached Canada became free.

CANADA'S ABOLITIONIST
SOCIETIES

In 1837, Canada's first major **abolitionist** society, called the Upper

Canada Anti-Slavery Society, was founded. Like many early abolitionist organizations in Canada, it did not last long. After the passage of the second Fugitive Slave Law in the United States in 1850, however, the Canadian abolitionist movement was revitalized. The new Fugitive Slave Law strengthened the first one and added further conditions. Now it was legal for Southern slaveholders to go into free states and claim their runaway "property." In addition, the new law required that all American citizens help capture runaway slaves. Any African American, free or enslaved, in any part of the United States, could be captured and sent into slavery.

In 1851, the Anti-Slavery Society of Canada was founded in Toronto by Canadian abolitionist George Brown (1818–1880). Brown was also the founder and editor of the *Toronto Globe*, a newspaper that he used to publish articles and editorials that attacked slavery in the United States. The *Globe* also featured speeches and announcements from the Anti-Slavery Society of Canada. On its first anniversary, the Anti-Slavery Society of Canada passed a resolution inviting fugitive slaves to Canada.

CANADA AND THE UNDERGROUND RAILROAD

From about 1820 to 1860, more than 20,000 escaping slaves fled the United States for Canada. The majority came to Upper Canada, which is now known as Ontario. The city of St. Catharine's in Ontario was the Canadian center of the Underground Railroad, and for many African Americans, it marked the end of a long journey out of the South. Some Underground Railroad routes led elsewhere in Canada, to cities such as Niagara Falls and Toronto. Some routes went as far east as Nova Scotia and as far west as British Columbia.

After the passage of the Fugitive Slave Law of 1850, thousands more African Americans traveled along the Underground Railroad and into Canada. Canadian abolitionists set up vigilance committees in cities both to help settle fugitive slaves and to protect them. Slave catchers were often sent from the South to kidnap free blacks in Canada and sell them into slavery. Slaveholders also tried to reclaim their "property" either by force or by bringing lawsuits against fugitive slaves in Canada. Vigilance committees helped defend fugitive slaves against their former owners.

SETTLING IN CANADA

Many fugitive slaves arriving in Upper Canada settled near the border and looked for work there. Very few came with money or skills; most arrived with just the clothes on their backs. Over time, some free African Americans earned enough money to move to larger cities like Toronto, and others bought their own small farms. Although many cities and towns in Canada supported abolitionism, many Canadians, faced with the growing numbers of African Americans moving in, became worried that free blacks would take jobs away from white residents. Just as they did in the United States, many free blacks in Canada faced **discrimination**. Despite this, however, there were a number of successful individuals and businesses in free black communities throughout Canada during the 1800s.

Josiah Henson (1789–1883) was born into slavery in Maryland and escaped to Ontario on the Underground Railroad in 1830. Henson began work on the Underground Railroad himself, helping more than 100 slaves escape from Kentucky to Canada. He also founded a 200-acre settlement for fugitive slaves in Dawn Township near Ontario, which included a manual-labor school. Henson published his autobiography in 1849 entitled *The Life of Josiah Henson, Formerly a Slave, Now an Inhabitant of Canada, as Narrated by Himself.* Author and abolitionist Harriet Beecher Stowe (1811–1896) read Henson's book, and his story inspired her to write the most famous antislavery novel of the nineteenth century, *Uncle Tom's Cabin.*

In 1863, during the Civil War (1861–1865), Abraham Lincoln (1861–1865) issued the Emancipation Proclamation, which freed slaves in those areas not under Union control and also permitted free blacks to join the Union Army for the first time. Many former slaves in Canada returned to the United States to help fight the Confederacy, though the majority stayed in their already established communities and continued to contribute to Canadian society.

See also: Emancipation Proclamation; Fugitive Slave Law; Gradualism; Slave Narratives; Slavery; Tubman, Harriet; *Uncle Tom's Cabin;* Underground Railroad.

FURTHER READING
Drew, Benjamin. *Refugees from Slavery: Autobiographies of Fugitive Slaves in Canada.* Pecos, N.Mex.: Dover Publications, 2004.

Clay, Henry (1777–1852)

Member of the U.S. Senate and House of Representatives from Kentucky, Speaker of the House, and secretary of state. Henry Clay was born on a farm in Virginia in 1777. At age 20, Clay became a lawyer and moved to Lexington, Kentucky, to practice law. He quickly established himself as a successful lawyer, a powerful speaker, and a great compromiser.

EARLY POLITICAL CAREER
Henry Clay's political career began in 1803 when he was elected to the Kentucky General Assembly. Three years later, he was elected U.S. senator from Kentucky. In 1808, he was chosen Speaker of the House of Representatives, and in 1810, he returned to the Senate. However, later that year he was elected again to the House of Representatives and became Speaker of the House, a position he was elected to five more times over the next 14 years.

THE MISSOURI COMPROMISE
In 1820, Henry Clay became famous for settling a dispute in Congress over slavery. It would later earn him the nicknames of "The Great Pacificator" and "The Great Compromiser." In 1818, the **territory** of Missouri applied for statehood as a slave state, which, if granted, would upset the equal balance of free states and slave states in the Senate. When Maine,

which was then a part of Massachusetts, applied for statehood the following year, Clay saw an opportunity for compromise.

Though a **slaveholder** himself, Henry Clay supported gradualism, or the slow but steady abolition of slavery. Clay knew, however, that the South would never agree to end slavery in Missouri, even if it was gradual. He felt that both sides should have to give up something or a decision would never be reached. Therefore, Clay proposed what became known as the Missouri Compromise. He recommended that Maine not be admitted to the Union as a free state unless Missouri was admitted as a slave state at the same time. This would keep the balance in the U.S. Senate. The Missouri Compromise also drew an imaginary line at the 36°30′ **parallel** north; all territory north of this line would be free, and all territory below the line would allow slavery.

THE COMPROMISE OF 1850

In 1850, Henry Clay once again proved his skills as the Great Compromiser. That year, Congress was faced with a number of important issues regarding slavery that threatened to divide the Union. The biggest question involved the **Mexican Cession,** the huge piece of land that the United States had recently acquired from Mexico. Congress argued over whether it should be a free or slave territory. In addition, California asked Congress to enter the Union as a free state, which would create a free-state majority in the Senate. There was also the question of the ac-tive slave trade in Washington, D.C., the capital of the United States. A final issue involved the state of Texas, which claimed that its western border stretched all the way into what is now New Mexico.

In January 1850, Henry Clay offered a compromise that he hoped would resolve all these issues. Clay proposed that the new territories in the West be allowed to determine for themselves if slavery should exist. He proposed that the slave trade, but not slavery, be abolished in Washington, D.C., and that Texas give up the territory it claimed in exchange for $10 million. Clay also proposed that California be admitted as a free state, but to balance it out, he proposed a stronger Fugitive Slave Law that required runaway slaves to be returned to their owners, no matter where they were found.

The final attempt In a famous speech on February 6, 1850, Clay argued that keeping the Union together made compromise a necessity. Clay said, "I implore . . . that if the direful and sad event of the dissolution of the Union shall happen, I may not survive to behold the sad and heart-rending spectacle."

Henry Clay died in 1852, nine years before the start of the Civil War (1861–1865). In his will, Clay freed the slaves on his Kentucky plantation.

See also: Adams, John Quincy; Compromise of 1850; Congress, United States; Fugitive Slave Law; Gradualism; Missouri Compromise (1820); Webster, Daniel.

FURTHER READING

Forbes, Robert Pierce. *The Missouri Compromise and Its Aftermath: Slavery and the Meaning of America.* Chapel Hill: University of North Carolina Press, 2007.

Hamilton, Holman. *Prologue to Conflict: The Crisis and Compromise of 1850.* Lexington: University Press of Kentucky, 2005.

Remini, Robert V. *Henry Clay: Statesman for the Union.* New York: W.W. Norton & Company, 1993.

Coffin, Levi

See Quakers.

Compromise of 1850

A series of five bills passed by Congress in September 1850. The bills were an attempt to reach a compromise over the expansion of slavery in the United States. President Millard Fillmore (1850–1853) signed the bills into law that same month.

THE ISSUES

By 1850, Congress was faced with a number of important issues regarding slavery, all of which threatened to divide the country. Thirty years earlier, the Missouri Compromise of 1820 had established a borderline of where slavery could be allowed in the new **territories** of the United States. After the Mexican-American War (1846–1848), however, the United States acquired 525,000 square miles (1.36 million square km) of territory from Mexico, which included present-day California, Nevada, and Utah, and parts of Arizona, New Mexico, and Colorado. Once again, North and South confronted the question of whether or not to allow slavery into the new territories.

In 1846, Pennsylvania representative David Wilmot proposed that slavery should be prohibited from any territory acquired from Mexico. Proslavery Southerners argued that Congress had no power to regulate slavery in the territories, and they rejected Wilmot's proposal, which became known as the **Wilmot Proviso.** The vote broke almost entirely along regional lines rather than partisan ones. Another proposal, by Illinois senator Stephen Douglas, was known as popular sovereignty. This proposal stated that settlers in a territory should decide whether or not to allow slavery. This, too, was rejected.

Congress debated other issues as well. California had petitioned Congress to enter the Union as a free state. If this happened, there would no longer be an equal balance of free and slave states, a balance that had been maintained since the Missouri Compromise of 1820. Southern senators refused to support California's admission to the Union.

Many Northerners in Congress also wanted to address the issue of slavery in Washington, D.C., the nation's capital. They believed that it sent a terrible message to the rest of the world that the capital of the United States allowed slavery and also had the largest slave market in the United States.

A final issue facing Congress involved the state of Texas, which claimed that its western border stretched all the way into what is now New Mexico. More than just a border decision, the outcome would affect slavery's reach into the territories.

THE DEBATE

In January 1850, Kentucky senator Henry Clay (1849–1852), nicknamed "The Great Compromiser" for his work on the Missouri Compromise, proposed yet another compromise that he hoped would resolve all these issues. Clay believed that Congress would have to address all the issues at once and that the North and South should each be willing to give up something in order to reach a compromise.

Clay proposed that the new territories of New Mexico and Utah determine for themselves if slavery should be allowed. He proposed the abolition of the slave trade in Washington, D.C., but not the abolition of slavery there. He also proposed that Texas give up its claim on western territory and accept $10 million from the federal government in compensation. Clay also proposed the admission of California as a free state. Knowing this would cause a free-state majority in the Senate, Clay proposed a stronger Fugitive Slave Law that would return runaway slaves to their owners, no matter where they were found.

As expected, opposition to Clay's compromise was fierce, and Congress debated over the proposals for eight months. South Carolina senator John Calhoun threatened his state's secession from the Union if the Compromise passed. Massachusetts senator Daniel Webster, known for his skills as a great speaker, gave a powerful speech in Congress in support of Clay's compromise. Many Northerners were outraged by Webster's support of the compromise, especially because they disapproved of the proposed Fugitive Slave Law. Yet Webster's speech reassured Southerners that since a Northern senator had backed Clay's proposal, Northerners might be willing to compromise.

President Zachary Taylor (1849–1850), a Southerner and a **slaveholder,** let it be known that he would not support the compromise. Taylor felt that any new territory should apply for statehood before the question of slavery was even addressed, and said that he would use force if any state tried to secede from the Union. Then, suddenly, in July 1850, Taylor died and Millard Fillmore (1850–1853) became the new president. President Fillmore supported the compromise. Even so, the Senate rejected it in a vote on July 31.

THE COMPROMISE

Finally, Senator Stephen Douglas came up with a solution. Instead of putting all the issues together into a single bill, Douglas introduced Clay's proposals in five separate bills. That way, he could get support from Northerners and Southerners on each issue. Most Northerners supported California entering the United States as a free state, the ending of the slave trade in the nation's capital, and the $10 million payment to Texas. Some Northern Democrats and all Southerners supported the stronger Fugitive Slave Law, as well as allowing settlers in the remaining territories to decide for themselves whether or not to allow slavery.

At the final vote in September 1850, only four senators and 28 representatives voted for every proposal. However, there were enough votes for each proposal, and they all passed. The final Compromise of 1850 stated that:

- California could enter the Union as a free state.
- The settlers of the New Mexico and Utah territories could decide for themselves whether to allow slavery or not.
- Texas would give up its land claims in present-day New Mexico, in exchange for $10 million.
- The slave trade, but not slavery, would be abolished in the District of Columbia.
- The Fugitive Slave Law would return escaped slaves to their owners and impose fines for federal officials who did not arrest runaway slaves.

Like the Missouri Compromise, the Compromise of 1850 kept the country from dividing, but it was only a temporary solution. Northerners were so angered by the Fugitive Slave Law that it was impossible to work out any future compromises. Over the next 10 years, Americans would become even more divided over the issue of slavery. This would ultimately result in the Civil War (1861–1865).

See also: Clay, Henry; Fugitive Slave Law; Missouri Compromise; Taylor, Zachary; Webster, Daniel.

FURTHER READING
Hamilton, Holman. *Prologue to Conflict: The Crisis and Compromise of 1850.* Lexington: University Press of Kentucky, 2005.

Congress, United States

Legislative branch of the U.S. government, consisting of two houses—the Senate and the House of Representatives—whose members are elected. Each member of the House of Representatives represents a district in his or her state. The number of representatives in each state is dependent upon that state's population, meaning that states with large populations have more representatives than states with small populations.

Today, there are 435 representatives in Congress, and they serve two-year terms. Each state also has two senators, regardless of that state's population. Today, there are 100 senators from the 50 states. Senators serve six-year terms.

HOW CONGRESS MAKES LAWS
The U.S. Congress makes the laws for the country. However, laws can only be enacted when both houses of Congress approve them and the president signs them. A law begins as a bill, which may be introduced by a member of either the Senate or House of Representatives. Committees review most bills. Once a committee approves a bill, it is introduced to the entire house, where it is debated and sometimes **amended.** Finally, the bill is voted upon. If the majority of the members in that house approve the bill, it passes.

After a bill passes in one house, it goes through the same procedure in the other house. If any amendments to the bill are made, the other house must approve the changes. After a bill passes in both houses, it is submitted to the president. The president may then choose to sign the bill, which makes it a law. The president may also choose to **veto** the bill and return it to Congress. In the case of a veto, a bill can only become a law if each house of Congress votes to override the veto with a two-thirds majority.

CONGRESS AND THE ISSUE OF SLAVERY

During the early 1800s, the U.S. Congress debated important issues that had huge impacts upon the growing nation. One of these issues was slavery. Because the population in each state determined the number of representatives in Congress, the question of how to count slaves was first debated during the writing of the Constitution in 1787. Northerners wanted to count only the free people in each state. However, Southerners wanted to include slaves in the population of slaveholding states. As a compromise, the Constitution established that slaves would be counted as "three-fifths" of a person. This gave the South an advantage because a part of the slave population was counted for purposes of representation; thus, on close votes in the House, the additional representatives often affected the passage of various laws regarding slavery.

As more **territories** applied for statehood in the early 1800s, the question of whether or not they should allow slavery was a topic of great debate in Congress. As long as there were an equal number of free states and slave states, there was always an equal number of senators in Congress. Because the North had a greater population, the South always had fewer representatives in Con-

gress, even with the three-fifths count. This meant that Southerners in Congress were adamant about not allowing additional free states into the Union. At the same time, however, Southerners usually held most major positions in the federal government up to the time of the Civil War (1861–1865)—president, Speaker of the House, president pro tem in the Senate, and a majority of the Supreme Court justices. If Southerners did not hold those offices outright, often sympathetic Northerners did. As a result, compromise became an important part of American politics during this period.

Compromise In 1820, the passage of the Missouri Compromise kept the balance between slave and free states by admitting Missouri as a slave state and Maine as a free state. In addition, Congress agreed to draw a borderline at the southern boundary of Missouri that would determine whether future states would allow slavery or be classified as free.

After the Mexican-American War (1846–1848), the United States acquired a huge territory from Mexico. Once again, Congress resorted to compromise when faced with the issue of whether or not to allow slavery into the new territories. One such compromise of significance was the Compromise of 1850, which admitted California as a free state and allowed the settlers of New Mexico to decide whether or not to allow slavery in the territory. This type of decision-making process is known as popular sovereignty.

The Kansas-Nebraska Act Just four years later, Congress passed the Kansas-Nebraska Act, which established that the territories of Kansas and Nebraska could also follow the idea of popular sovereignty to resolve the issue of whether they would allow slavery. Violence soon broke out between antislavery and proslavery settlers in Kansas, as well as proslavery Missourians from across the border. Congress finally recognized that compromise was an unsatisfactory solution to the problem of slavery in the United States. Ultimately, the struggle in the country between North and South, free states and slave states, would lead to Civil War. In 1865, the end of the war finally brought about the abolition of slavery in the United States.

See also: Clay, Henry; Compromise of 1850; Kansas-Nebraska Act; Missouri Compromise; Popular Sovereignty; Republican Party and Abolitionism; Taylor, Zachary; Webster, Daniel.

FURTHER READING

Schulman, Bruce J., ed. *Student's Guide to Congress.* Washington, D.C.: CQ Press, 2009.

D–E

Douglas, Stephen A.

See Lincoln-Douglas Debates; Popular Sovereignty.

Douglass, Frederick (1818–1895)

African American **abolitionist,** author, publisher, lecturer, and statesman. Frederick Douglass was born into slavery in 1818 on a farm in Maryland. Douglass's mother was a slave on the farm, and all he knew about his father was that he was white.

EARLY LIFE

When Douglass was about eight, he was sent to Baltimore to work as a houseboy in the home of Hugh and Sophia Auld, who were relatives of his master. Soon after Douglass arrived, Sophia Auld began to teach him the alphabet, despite the fact that it was illegal to teach slaves to read. When Hugh Auld found out, he forbade his wife to continue, but Douglass read secretly whenever he could. Later, Douglass said, "Going to live in Baltimore laid the foundation, and opened the gateway, to all my subsequent prosperity."

ESCAPE FROM SLAVERY

In 1836, at the age of 18, Douglass decided to escape from slavery by way of a plan he worked out with five other slaves. Unfortunately, the plan was discovered, and the men were put into jail for a week. Two years later, Douglass was determined to escape again. On September 3, 1838, he bought a train ticket to Philadelphia, using money he borrowed from his fiancée, Anna Murray, a free black woman. Douglass dressed as a sailor and borrowed a free black seaman's identification papers. Douglass reached Philadelphia that night and then took a train to New York City. He was free at last. Douglass married Anna Murray, and the couple moved to New Bedford, Massachusetts. There, Douglass began to attend abolitionist meetings. He also subscribed to William Lloyd Garrison's (1805–1879) weekly abolitionist newspaper, *The Liberator.*

ABOLITIONIST

In 1841, Douglass saw Garrison speak at the Bristol Anti-Slavery Society's annual meeting. Later, Douglass explained that "no face and form ever impressed me with such sentiments as did those of William Lloyd Garrison." Garrison was also impressed by Douglass's eloquence at the meeting. A week later, Garrison asked Douglass to speak at a convention of the Massachusetts Anti-Slavery Society in **Nantucket.** It was Douglass's first official lecture, and, though he was uncomfortable addressing a white audience, all who attended the meeting were impressed by his intelligence, sharp wit, and manner of speaking.

Realizing that the firsthand account of a former slave would be especially effective to the abolitionist cause, Garrison and others encouraged Douglass to continue as an anti-

An 1885 portrait of Frederick Douglass shows the abolitionist at about age 68. Douglass escaped from slavery in 1838 and made his way to the North, where he eventually became a passionate speaker for freeing the slaves.

slavery lecturer. That fall, Douglass was asked to be an agent of the Massachusetts Anti-Slavery Society and he embarked on a lecture tour that lasted three years.

During his lectures, Douglass was careful not to mention the specifics of his escape or to give the real names of his owners. Because he was a **fugitive** slave, Douglass was still legally bound to his master and could be sent back to slavery at any time.

However, because Douglass's accounts lacked specific details, many in his audience began to question if he had ever really been enslaved. In addition, as Douglass later wrote, "People . . . said I did not talk like a slave, look like a slave, nor act like a slave. . . ."

In 1845, Douglass wrote an autobiography called *Narrative of the Life of Frederick Douglass, an American Slave, Written by Himself.* The book discussed the specifics of his life as a slave and his escape. After its publication, Douglass spent two years on a lecture tour in Great Britain. He made the trip with the main purpose of encouraging the British to support the American antislavery cause, but he also went on the trip to avoid bounty hunters who might send him back to his master. While in Great Britain, some of his friends paid Douglass's former master for his freedom.

THE NORTH STAR

When Douglass returned to the United States in 1847, he began to publish his own abolitionist newspaper, called the *North Star*, out of Rochester, New York. Ever since Douglass had first met William Lloyd Garrison, Garrison had been a mentor to him. Like Garrison, Douglass supported immediatism, or the immediate end to slavery and the immediate establishment of equal rights for African Americans. Nevertheless, during his time abroad, Douglass's views about the American abolitionist movement had begun to change. Garrison was considered the most radical of all abolitionist leaders. He believed that the free states of the Union should break away and form their own country. He rejected the U.S. Constitution, calling it a proslavery document. He felt that abolitionism was a moral issue and did not think it appropriate to use politics to achieve it. Garrison was also a **pacifist,** who believed that the end of slavery should only be achieved peacefully.

Douglass, however, did not believe that the Constitution was a proslavery document, but thought it could be used to help end slavery. Douglass also did not support the idea of breaking up the Union because it would not help the slaves in the South. Douglass supported nonviolence to achieve freedom, but he believed that slaves should be able to use self-defense if necessary. Finally, Douglass believed that politics was a useful tool when it came to attacking the institution of slavery. Both Douglass and Garrison wrote about their divergent views in their newspapers, sometimes criticizing each other. Their relationship was never the same. By that time, however, Douglass had become the most respected African American leader in the country.

FINAL YEARS

During the 1850s, Douglass's home in Rochester became a stop on the Underground Railroad, a secret network of safe houses that helped runaway slaves escape. During the Civil War (1861–1865), Douglass met with President Abraham Lincoln (1861–1865), first to request that African Americans be given the opportunity to become Union soldiers, and later to request improvements of the conditions for African American soldiers. After the war, Douglass fought for the voting rights of African American men, which were granted in 1870 after the ratification of the Fifteenth Amendment. In his last years, Douglass served as U.S. Marshal for the District of Columbia and minister-general to the Republic of Haiti. Douglass died in 1895 at the age of 77.

See also: Emancipation Proclamation; Garrison, William Lloyd; Immediatism; The *North Star*; Slave Narratives; *The Liberator;* Underground Railroad.

FURTHER READING

Burchard, Peter. *Frederick Douglass: For the Great Family of Man*. New York: Simon and Schuster, 2007.

Douglass, Frederick. *The Narrative of the Life of Frederick Douglass, An American Slave, Written by Himself*. New York: Barnes and Noble Classics, 2005.

Dred Scott Decision (1857)

A ruling by the U.S. Supreme Court declaring that all African Americans, enslaved or free, were not and could never become citizens of the United States. It also ruled that Congress had no authority to prohibit slavery in U.S. **territories.**

Dred Scott was an enslaved African American who had been purchased by Dr. John Emerson, a military surgeon in Missouri, in 1830. During the course of his work, Dr. Emerson lived in the free state of Illinois and the free territory of Wisconsin; Dred Scott accompanied him.

In 1842, Scott returned with the Emersons to Missouri. Four years later, after Dr. Emerson died, Scott sued for his freedom in court, claiming that, because he had lived for almost nine years in free territories, he should be free. In 1847, the case first went to trial, and a jury determined that Dred Scott should be free. But Dr. Emerson's wife appealed the case to the Missouri Supreme Court, which in 1852 reversed the ruling.

Working with a team of **abolitionist** lawyers, Dred Scott continued to fight for his freedom. In 1854, he sued in Federal Court against John Sanford, Dr. Emerson's brother-in-law, who was executor of the estate. Sanford won, but Dred Scott appealed the case again, this time to the U.S. Supreme Court. The case was *Dred Scott v. Sanford.*

On March 6, 1857, seven of the nine Supreme Court justices ruled that Dred Scott should remain enslaved. The Supreme Court's decision was written by Chief Justice Roger B. Taney, a former **slaveholder** from Maryland. Taney wrote that African Americans were not intended by the framers of the Declaration of Independence to be included as citizens of the new nation. Because no slave or descendant of a slave could be, or could ever have been, a U.S. citizen, they could not sue in a federal court.

Dred Scott's defense had been that the Missouri Compromise of 1820, which prohibited slavery in territories north of the **parallel** 36°30′, guaranteed his freedom. In its ruling, however, Taney declared that the Missouri Compromise was unconstitutional. The Fifth Amendment of the Constitution prohibits Congress from depriving people of their property without due process of law. Because slaves were considered property, the majority of Supreme Court justices felt that the Constitution protected slaveholders' rights. As a result, slavery was to be permitted in all federal territories.

The *Dred Scott* decision affected every African American living in the United States, free or enslaved. Chief Justice Taney ruled that even free blacks could never be U.S. citizens. At the time, free African American males had been able to vote in seven Northern states. Some had even held public office. Yet Taney declared that, even if an African American was a citizen of a state, "it does not by any means follow . . . that he must be a citizen of the United States."

The American public reacted strongly to the *Dred Scott* decision. Southerners approved it because they believed that Congress had no right to prohibit slavery in the territories. Abolitionist leaders in the North were outraged, convinced that Southerners were intending to extend slavery throughout the nation. Two months after the *Dred Scott* decision, free African American and abolitionist Frederick Douglass delivered a speech before the American Abolition Society. He declared that his "hopes were never brighter than now." He believed that the *Dred Scott* decision would anger enough Americans to motivate them to action. Douglass saw the decision as the beginning of the end of slavery. He explained: "This very attempt to blot out forever the hopes of an enslaved people may be one necessary link in the chain of events preparatory to the downfall

and complete overthrow of the whole slave system."

The Republican Party, which was founded in 1854 to prohibit the spread of slavery into the Western territories, was motivated by the *Dred Scott* decision to fight harder for control of Congress. Former U.S. Representative Abraham Lincoln returned to politics after the *Dred Scott* decision, speaking out strongly against the Court's ruling. Overall, the *Dred Scott* decision served to further divide the North and the South over the question of slavery, and it brought the United States closer to war.

In 2009, in the city of Frederick, Maryland, a bronze plaque was erected to educate visitors about the Dred Scott decision. The plaque stands just eight feet away from a statue of one-time Frederick resident Chief Justice Taney, who wrote the controversial decision.

See also: American Abolition Society; Douglass, Frederick; Lincoln-Douglass Debates; Missouri Compromise.

FURTHER READING
Simon, James F. *Lincoln and Chief Justice Taney: Slavery, Secession, and the President's War Powers.* New York: Simon and Schuster, 2006.

Emancipation Proclamation (1863)

Order issued by President Abraham Lincoln (1861–1865) and signed on January 1, 1863, in the middle of the Civil War (1861–1865). It declared the end of slavery in all areas not under control of the Union. Today, the Emancipation Proclamation is considered the first step to the end of slavery in the United States.

THE CIVIL WAR BEGINS

During the 1860 presidential election, many states in the South threatened to **secede** from the Union if Republican candidate Abraham Lincoln won. The Republican Party had been founded in 1854 in response to the Kansas-Nebraska Act and sought to prevent the expansion of slavery into the Western territories. Southerners feared that a Republican in the White House would mean the abolition of slavery throughout the United States.

By the time Lincoln was inaugurated as president, in March 1861, seven Southern states had already seceded from the Union. Lincoln was concerned that more would follow. In his **inaugural address,** Lincoln announced that he had "no purpose, directly or indirectly, to interfere with the institution of slavery in the States where it exists. I believe I have no lawful right to do so, and I have no inclination to do so." He also pledged to enforce the Fugitive Slave Law of 1850, which made it legal for **slaveholders** to hunt down and capture escaped African Americans and send them back into slavery.

Lincoln's message did not satisfy the South. A month later, the first shots were fired at the Battle of Fort Sumter in South Carolina, beginning the Civil War. Four more Southern states quickly seceded from the Union. Five slave states—Delaware, Maryland, Kentucky, Missouri, and, later, West Virginia—did not leave the Union during the Civil War. They were known as **border states,** and

throughout the war, the South tried to persuade them to join the Southern cause.

DEMAND FOR ABOLITION

At the start of the Civil War, many Republicans in Congress demanded that President Lincoln issue a proclamation that would end slavery in the United States. American abolitionist leaders, such as William Lloyd Garrison (1805–1879) and free African American Frederick Douglass (1818–1895), also criticized Lincoln for not addressing slavery at the start of the war. Douglass said, "The American people and the Government at Washington may refuse to recognize it for a time; but the 'inexorable logic of events' will force it upon them in the end; that the war as waged in this land is a war for and against slavery." However, Lincoln refused to issue a proclamation that ended slavery, explaining that his main concern was to preserve the Union. He also pointed out that, if he abolished slavery at this point, some or all of the border states would secede and join the South.

As the war continued and as it became clear that it would not be an easy victory for either side, more Northerners became open to the idea that Lincoln free the slaves. Some were against slavery simply because they believed it was wrong. Others wanted to punish Southern slaveholders and felt that freeing the slaves would be a good way to disrupt the Southern economy during the war. On August 19, 1862, Horace Greeley (1811–1872), the editor of the New York *Tribune*, published in his newspaper an open letter to President

Lincoln entitled "The Prayer of Twenty Millions." It demanded that Lincoln free the slaves.

Three days later, Lincoln issued a reply to Greeley's editorial. He again stressed his most important goal for the war: "My paramount object in this struggle is to save the Union, and is not either to save or to destroy slavery. If I could save the Union without freeing any slave I would do it, and if I could save it by freeing all slaves I would do it. . . . What I do about slavery . . . I do because I believe it helps to save the Union. . . ."

THE PROCLAMATION

Yet, unbeknownst to most Americans, a month earlier Lincoln had written a **preliminary** Emancipation Proclamation that freed slaves in the seceded Southern states not under control of Union forces. He shared this preliminary proclamation with his cabinet. Secretary of State William Seward advised Lincoln to wait to issue it until after a Union victory in the war, so that it would not look like a desperate act on his part. On September 17, 1862, the Union side narrowly won at the Battle of Antietam in Maryland. Lincoln felt that the time was right to act. Five days later, he issued his preliminary Emancipation Proclamation, which announced that beginning January 1, 1863, "all persons held as slaves within any State or designated part of a State in which the people whereof shall then be in rebellion against the United States shall be then, thenceforward, and forever free."

After the preliminary Emancipation Proclamation was shared with the American public, Lincoln did not feel optimistic about its response. He wrote in a letter, "It is six days old, and while commendation in newspapers and by distinguished individuals is all that a vain man could wish, the stocks have declined, and troops come forward more slowly than ever. This, looked soberly in the face, is not very satisfactory." Lincoln gave the Southern states until the end of the year to rejoin the Union if they wanted to keep slavery in their states. All refused to do so. On January 1, 1863, Lincoln issued the final Emancipation Proclamation. As he signed the document, Lincoln was quoted as saying, "I never, in my life, felt more certain that I was doing right, than I do in signing this paper."

THE WAR'S FOCUS CHANGES

However, there is some debate over what the Emancipation Proclamation actually accomplished, especially within the first few days of its signing. The document was worded very carefully, and it did not free all the slaves living in the United States at the time. It did not free the slaves in the border states because these states were not in rebellion against the Union. In addition, even in those Southern states that had seceded, it was not immediately possible to enforce the order because the state governments there refused to acknowledge any orders issued from President Lincoln—though that would change as the Union armies took control of more Southern territory. Nor did the proclamation free slaves in areas of the South already under Union control—New Orleans, for instance. For these reasons, many people have claimed that the Emancipation Proclamation did not really free a single slave. Even Secretary of State Seward commented, "We show our sympathy with slavery by emancipating slaves where we cannot reach them and holding them in bondage where we can set them free."

Although at first the Emancipation Proclamation affected only those slaves who had already escaped to the Union side, as the war continued and the Union won more battles and took control of larger areas of the South, thousands of slaves were freed each day. Sometimes the Union army freed them, and sometimes the slaves ran to the army and freed themselves. In either case, nothing would have happened without the aid of the Emancipation Proclamation. The end of the war liberated 4 million slaves.

The Emancipation Proclamation is considered a turning point of the Civil War. As Lincoln had insisted, from the start the war had been about restoring the Union, but now it had also become the war that would finally put an end to slavery. Although the Emancipation Proclamation

D–E

Freedom and Voting Rights

Before the Civil War, a few Northern states allowed free black men to vote. In practice, restrictive state laws and slavery meant that very few African Americans actually voted. In 1870, the Fifteenth Amendment gave African American men the right to vote. As a result, hundreds of thousands of recently freed slaves in the South registered to vote.

Still, the African American citizen's right to vote was strongly resisted in the South. Terrorist groups such as the Ku Klux Klan used violence and intimidation to keep African Americans from the polls. By the 1890s, many Southern states amended their constitutions and enacted a series of laws to prevent African Americans from voting. As a result, by 1910, nearly all African Americans in the South had lost the right to vote.

It was not until 1965 that a law passed to guarantee African Americans the rights granted to them by the Fifteenth Amendment. Although there were federal antidiscrimination laws in place, many Southern state governments overrode these with their own discriminatory legislation. President Lyndon B. Johnson (1963–1969) signed the Voting Rights Act into law in August 1965. The act prohibited any American citizen from being denied the right to vote. It also allowed for federal observers to monitor suspect polling places to ensure that no one interfered with registration and voting.

The Voting Rights Act was extended in 1970, 1975, and 1982; in 2006, amendments were added to protect non-English-speaking citizens from voter discrimination. Many people consider the Voting Rights Act the most successful law ever passed by Congress.

The Voting Rights Act and its extensions have allowed more American citizens to participate in the democratic processes, helping to ensure that "We the people" have a say in the nation's government.

depended upon a Union victory to truly free all the slaves in the United States, it was the beginning of the end of slavery. The Emancipation Proclamation also permitted free African Americans to fight as Union soldiers for the first time. Now African Americans could take part in the war for their own freedom.

The Emancipation Proclamation changed Lincoln's focus for the war as well. He clearly expressed what it had now come to mean to him in a letter written in March 1864 to Albert Hodges, editor of the *Frankfort Commonwealth* newspaper in Kentucky: "If slavery is not wrong, nothing is wrong. I can not remember when I did not so think, and feel. And yet I have never understood that the Presidency conferred upon me an unrestricted right to act officially upon this judgment and feeling. . . . Now, at the end of three years' struggle the nation's condition is not what either party, or any man devised, or expected." Lincoln had by then realized that, in order to put the Union back together, the question of slavery had to be addressed once and for all.

THE PUBLIC'S REACTION

Americans reacted to the Emancipation Proclamation in different ways. As predicted, most Southerners simply rejected it. Some Northerners opposed the Emancipation Proclamation because they supported the institution of slavery and did not think it should be abolished. Others feared that freed slaves would rush into the cities and towns of the North and take jobs away from whites. On the other hand, some Northerners felt

Lincoln had not gone far enough with his proclamation. They felt that he should have abolished slavery everywhere and not have allowed it to remain in the border states.

Enslaved African Americans were thrilled when the news of the Emancipation Proclamation reached them, and many celebrations were held. As the war progressed, increasing numbers of slaves escaped to Northern states once they realized that freedom was possible. Many joined the Union army and served in all-black regiments. By the end of the war, almost 200,000 African Americans had fought for the Union side as soldiers and sailors.

However, not all African American slaves in the South knew that they were free. The most striking example of this was seen in Texas, where the news of the Emancipation Proclamation did not reach the slaves there until June 1865, two-and-a-half years after it was issued, and two months after the Civil War had officially ended. Union General Gordon Granger and his troops arrived in Galveston, Texas, on June 19, to declare the end of the war and to inform the slaves there of their freedom. This led to a special celebration in Texas that came to be remembered every year. This date in history, which is known as **Juneteenth,** is still celebrated today as a national Independence Day for African Americans.

FREEDOM FOR ALL

Abraham Lincoln's Emancipation Proclamation was considered the beginning of the end of slavery for a number of reasons. One reason was that, as president, Lincoln had no constitutional right to end the institution of slavery in the United States. The Emancipation Proclamation was actually a war action issued by Lincoln, who as president was also commander in chief. Lincoln and many Republicans in Congress realized that, to truly abolish slavery in the United States, the Emancipation Proclamation would have to be followed by an **amendment** to the U.S. Constitution.

In March 1864, Illinois senator Lyman Trumball helped draft a proposed Thirteenth Amendment to the U.S. Constitution that would abolish slavery. The following month, it was presented to Congress, where it easily passed in the Senate but did not get the required two-thirds majority in the House of Representatives.

President Lincoln soon took an active role in encouraging the passage of the Thirteenth Amendment. He insisted that its passage be added to the Republican Party platform for the upcoming presidential election, calling the new amendment "a fitting and necessary conclusion to the final success of the Union cause." Lincoln won the 1864 election, which was held during the war and without the participation of the 11 states that had seceded from the Union. During a speech at the last session of Congress in December 1864, Lincoln urged all the members to vote for the Thirteenth Amendment.

In January 1865, the House of Representatives voted again on the Thirteenth Amendment, and this time, it passed. When Congress sent the amendment to Lincoln for his signature, he reportedly said, "This amendment is a King's cure for all the evils. It winds the whole thing up." By December 18, 1865, three-fourths, or 27 of the 36 states, ratified the Thirteenth Amendment so that it became part of the Constitution. What had once begun as a war action nearly three years earlier was now a law. Slavery had finally been prohibited forever from the United States.

See also: Douglass, Frederick; Garrison, William Lloyd; Gradualism; Republican Party and Abolitionism; Slavery; Thirteenth Amendment.

F–G

Fillmore, Millard

See Compromise of 1850; Taylor, Zachary.

Fugitive Slave Law (1850)

One of five **bills** that passed as part of the Compromise of 1850. The Fugitive Slave Law was considered the most controversial of the bills. It was created because one of the five bills admitted California to the Union as a free state. Kentucky senator Henry Clay, author of the Compromise of 1850, felt that in order for Southerners in Congress to approve another free state in the Union, they needed a bill that strengthened slavery in the South. The new Fugitive Slave Law reinforced the first Fugitive Slave Law that Congress had passed in 1793 and which had only been loosely enforced in the North.

CHANGES TO THE FIRST FUGITIVE SLAVE LAW

The first Fugitive Slave Law made it illegal for anyone in the United States to help runaway slaves or prevent their arrest. The Fugitive Slave Law of 1850 went much further. Now it was legal for Southern **slaveholders** to go into free states and claim their runaway "property." In addition, the new law required all American citizens to help capture runaway slaves. Anyone who refused to help capture runaways or was caught assisting or hiding a runaway slave would be subject to large fines and even imprisonment. U.S. marshals were ordered to hunt for runaway slaves and return them to their rightful owners. If a marshal refused, he would be fined $1,000.

The new Fugitive Slave Law also took away runaway slaves' most basic legal rights. They were denied the right to a jury trial and the right to testify in their own defense. All that was necessary for a slaveholder to "prove" ownership of an African American was for the slaveholder to

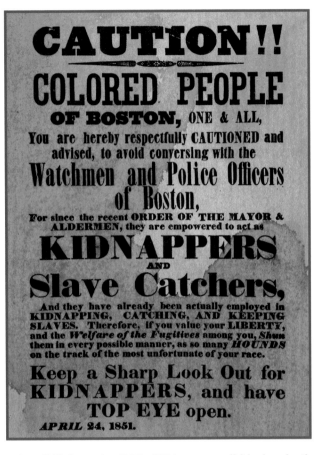

A handbill from April 24, 1851, warns all blacks—both free African Americans and runaway slaves—living in Boston to be aware of slave catchers in the area. This warning was posted after a runaway slave had been forcibly returned to Georgia from Boston, an action made legal following the enactment of the 1850 Fugitive Slave Act.

claim that the African American belonged to him. The African Americans in question were denied the opportunity to defend themselves.

The new law also made the process for filing claims against runaway slaves much easier for slaveholders. Special commissioners were hired to handle the claims of captured runaway slaves. The slaveholder was responsible for paying the commissioner

$5 if a fugitive slave was let go and $10 if he or she was returned to slavery. It was extremely rare for commissioners to allow runaways to remain free. Many **abolitionists** claimed that this part of the Fugitive Slave Law was merely a bribe for commissioners. It ensured that any African American accused of being a runaway would be found guilty and sent back to slavery.

RESPONSE TO THE FUGITIVE SLAVE LAW

The Fugitive Slave Law of 1850 was devastating. Any African American, enslaved or free, could be sent into slavery if someone claimed to be his or her owner. It had now become profitable for slaveholders to hire slave catchers to find and arrest suspected runaway slaves. Many former slaves who had been living freely in the North fled to Canada, where Southern slaveholders did not have the legal right to retrieve them. It is estimated that approximately 20,000 African Americans **migrated** to Canada between 1850 and 1860. Some African Americans who had been free their entire lives fled to Canada for fear of being sent into slavery. Harriet Jacobs (1813–1897), an escaped slave living in New York, described this time as "the beginning of a reign of terror to the colored population." Jacobs, whose autobiography was the first slave narrative written by a woman, remained in New York, even though slave catchers had been hired to track her down.

Underground Railroad The Underground Railroad, a secret network of safe houses and hiding places that had volunteers who helped runaway slaves escape to freedom, became the most active during this period, reaching a peak between 1850 and 1860. Because so many African Americans were captured and returned to slavery, the Underground Railroad maintained safe houses in free states as well as slave states to protect escaped slaves and to guide them farther north to Canada. Free black communities in the North also increased their aid to runaway slaves after the passage of the Fugitive Slave Law. They provided them with additional places to hide within their communities, including churches and homes, and established vigilance committees to protect African Americans from slave catchers who were sent to the North to search for runaway slaves.

More Northern opposition Most Northern state governments actively opposed the new Fugitive Slave Law. Between 1850 and 1859, eight Northern states passed Personal Liberty Laws, which prohibited state officials from assisting in the return of runaways to slaveholders. The laws also gave fugitive slaves the right to a jury trial. In 1859, the Supreme Court of Wisconsin declared the Fugitive Slave Law unconstitutional. Five years earlier, abolitionist Sherman Booth had freed a captured, fugitive slave from a jail in Milwaukee. Booth was accused of helping a fugitive slave escape, but the case went to the Wisconsin Supreme Court, where the Fugitive Slave Law had been declared unconstitutional. Later that year, the

U.S. Supreme Court reversed the Wisconsin decision and upheld the Fugitive Slave Law.

However, passage of the Fugitive Slave Law made abolitionists even more determined to end slavery in the United States. They had witnessed the brutality of slavery firsthand as they saw hundreds of African Americans kidnapped and forced back into slavery in the South. Many Northerners who had not voiced any objection to slavery now took a stand against it. In various cities throughout the North, vigilance committees, local abolition societies, African American churches, and individuals—both white and African American—all worked to help fugitive slaves, either to settle in cities and find work or to move farther North. The question of whether to allow slavery to extend farther into new territories acquired by the United States demanded an answer during the 1850s. The consequences of the Fugitive Slave Law made more Northerners determined to stop the spread of slavery in the United States.

When the Civil War (1861–1865) began, the Fugitive Slave Law remained in effect. In some cases, it was used to bring claims against African Americans who had escaped slavery in **border states** loyal to the Union. Both Fugitive Slave Laws were eventually repealed by Congress, but not until June 1864.

See also: Canada and the Abolitionist Movement; Clay, Henry; Compromise of 1850; Congress, United States; Slave Narratives; Slavery; Underground Railroad.

Gag Rule

See Adams, John Quincy.

Garrett, Thomas (1789–1871)

Iron merchant, **abolitionist**, and "stationmaster" on the Underground Railroad. In the early 1800s, Thomas Garrett's home in Wilmington, Delaware, was the last stop on the Underground Railroad before runaway slaves reached the free state of Pennsylvania. It is estimated that Garrett helped free more than 2,700 slaves. Author and abolitionist Harriet Beecher Stowe (1811–1896) used Thomas Garrett as the basis for the character Simeon Halliday in her popular antislavery novel *Uncle Tom's Cabin* (1852).

EARLY YEARS

Thomas Garrett was born in Pennsylvania in 1789. The Garretts were Quakers and, like most Quakers, believed that slavery was wrong. As a child, Garrett saw his parents hiding runaway slaves in their farmhouse. When Garrett was a young man, a family servant was kidnapped and forced into slavery. Garrett helped the woman escape, and from this incident, he decided to devote his life to the cause of abolitionism. Many Quakers believed that slavery should end, but Garrett took a more radical approach. He was a follower of abolitionist leader William Lloyd Garrison (1805–1879), who believed in immediatism, or the immediate end to slavery and the subsequent establishment of equal rights for African Americans.

STATIONMASTER

In 1822, Garrett moved to Wilmington and established an iron and hardware business there. Delaware, a slave state, was in many ways the dividing line between the North and South. Adjacent to the free states of Pennsylvania and New Jersey on one side, and the slave state of Maryland on the other, Delaware was a stop for many slaves on the Underground Railroad. Thomas Garrett was known as an important stationmaster on the eastern line of the Underground Railroad. Through various networks, many runaway slaves escaping from Maryland were directed to his house. There, Garrett gave them food and often a pair of shoes before smuggling them through the last 20 miles (32 km) of the slave states into the free state of Pennsylvania. Harriet Tubman (*c.* 1820–1913), who had escaped from a Maryland plantation, was a frequent guest at Garrett's house. After Tubman's own escape, she continued to cross back into Delaware to help other slaves reach freedom.

THOMAS GARRETT'S TRIAL

Thomas Garrett did not hide the fact that he was helping escaped slaves, and he was often threatened with violence by **slaveholders.** Garrett's work on the Underground Railroad was so well known that the neighboring state of Maryland offered a reward of $10,000 for his arrest. In 1848, Thomas Garrett and fellow abolitionist John Hunn were tried in court for helping a family in Maryland escape from slavery. According to the Fugitive Slave Act of 1793, it was illegal for anyone to help escaping slaves. Though it was known for years that Garrett helped slaves escape, this time he was being sued in court by slaveholders. The trial was presided over by U.S. Supreme Court Chief Justice Roger Taney, a former slaveholder from Maryland. Garrett and Hunn were found guilty and fined thousands of dollars.

In the courtroom, Garrett announced that he would continue to help runaway slaves as long they needed him. He declared: "Judge, thou hast left me not a dollar, but I wish to say to thee and to all in this courtroom that if any one knows a fugitive who wants a shelter and a friend, send him to Thomas Garrett and he will befriend him." The fines left Garrett **bankrupt,** but with help from abolitionist friends, Garrett was able to pay the fine and reestablish his business. He stayed true to his beliefs and continued to help slaves to freedom.

FINAL YEARS

In 1865, the Thirteenth Amendment to the Constitution abolished slavery in the United States. However, Thomas Garrett did not give up his fight for the rights of African Americans, and he did all he could to help former slaves. When the Fifteenth Amendment, which gave black men the right to vote, passed in 1870, the elderly Garrett was paraded through the streets of Wilmington by his supporters.

On January 25, 1871, Garrett died at the age of 81. Thousands of people, black and white, came to his funeral. As he requested, African American pallbearers carried Garrett's coffin on their shoulders to the Wilmington Friends Meeting House. William Lloyd Garrison, who was unable to attend the funeral, wrote to Garrett's son: "What he promised, he fulfilled; what he attempted, he seldom or never failed to accomplish; what he believed, he dared to proclaim upon the housetop; what he ardently desired and incessantly longed for was the reign of universal peace and righteousness."

See also: Fugitive Slave Law; Garrison, William Lloyd; Immediatism; Quakers; Slavery; Thirteenth Amendment; *Uncle Tom's Cabin;* Underground Railroad.

FURTHER READING

McGlowan, James A. *Station Master on the Underground Railroad: The Life and Letters of Thomas Garrett,* rev. ed. Jefferson, N.C.: McFarland, 2009.

Garrison, William Lloyd (1805–1879)

A leader in the American **abolitionist** movement and founding editor of the abolitionist newspaper *The Liberator.* William Lloyd Garrison was born in Newburyport, Massachusetts, in 1805. He received little formal schooling, but at the age of 13, he became an **apprentice** at the local *Herald.* There he learned printing and wrote anonymously for the paper. He eventually started his own antislavery newspaper, *The Liberator*, and became a strong supporter of immediatism, the movement to end slavery immediately.

ABOLITIONIST

After his apprenticeship ended in 1826, Garrison edited his own paper, the *Free Press,* which folded after two years. In 1828, Garrison moved to Boston to become editor of the *National Philanthropist,* the first American journal to promote **temperance.** It was there that he first read an issue of the *Genius of Universal Emancipation,* published by Quaker abolitionist Benjamin Lundy (1789–1839). The *Genius of Universal Emancipation* was the first American newspaper solely devoted to the antislavery cause. By then, Garrison had already committed himself to abolitionism. He quit his newspaper and the following year went to work as assistant editor for Benjamin Lundy's paper.

Not long after he began work on the *Genius of Universal Emancipation,* Garrison was sent to jail for **libel** after the newspaper attacked a Massachusetts merchant for allowing his ship to be used to transport slaves. However, Garrison had already begun to break away from Benjamin Lundy's beliefs. At the time, Lundy and most other American abolitionists supported gradualism, which called for the gradual end of slavery. Many abolitionists believed that slaves should be freed only after they were educated and more able to enter society. Others believed in **colonization**, which called for all free African Americans to be settled in colonies in Africa. Garrison at first supported the ideas of gradualism and colonization. Soon, though, he rejected both of these in favor of immediatism, or the immediate freeing of all slaves and the immediate establishment of equal rights for African Americans.

THE LIBERATOR

After Garrison was freed from jail, he returned to Boston, and on January 1, 1831, he published the first issue of his own weekly abolitionist newspaper, *The Liberator.* This newspaper made Garrison known throughout the country as a fervent abolitionist. Through *The Liberator,* Garrison attacked **slaveholders** and anyone who did not share his antislavery views. Garrison refused to tone down his harsh writing style. He wrote: "If those who deserve the lash feel it and wince at it, I shall be assured that I am striking the right persons in the right place." In 1832, he published a book called *Thoughts on Colonization,* which attacked the concept of colonization and accused its supporters of being racist. Yet despite his harsh words, Garrison did not believe in violence. He wrote that he wanted "nothing more than the peaceful abolition of slavery. . . ." Southerners, however, considered Garrison a real threat, and the state of Georgia even offered a $5,000 reward for his arrest.

ABOLITIONIST SOCIETIES

In 1832, Garrison founded the New England Anti-Slavery Society, the first immediatist society in the country. The following year, he helped organize the American Anti-Slavery Society, and wrote its Declaration of Sentiments based on the Declaration of Independence. Yet by 1839, the American Anti-Slavery Society had split into two groups. Some members found Garrison's beliefs too radical.

He supported not only African American rights but also women's rights. He also argued that the Constitution was a proslavery document and felt that the North should secede from the Union and become its own free country. Free African American abolitionist Frederick Douglass (1818–1895), once a great supporter of Garrison's, disagreed with Garrison on these issues. Douglass believed that the Constitution could actually be used as a weapon against slavery. This difference of opinion damaged their great friendship and working relationship.

FINAL YEARS

William Lloyd Garrison supported the Civil War (1861–1865) because he believed it could destroy slavery once and for all. He also publicly praised President Abraham Lincoln's (1861–1865) Emancipation Proclamation (1863), which freed all slaves in states that were in rebellion against the Union.

Garrison wrote his last editorial for *The Liberator* on December 29, 1865. He spent his last years in retirement, believing that he had fulfilled his life's work. However, he continued to support temperance, women's rights, and African American rights. William Lloyd Garrison died on May 24, 1879. At his memorial service, Garrison's friend Frederick Douglass was quoted as saying, "It was the glory of this man that he could stand alone with the truth, and calmly await the result."

See also: American Anti-Slavery Society; Douglass, Frederick; Emancipation Proclamation; Gradualism; Immediatism; *Liberator, The*; Quakers.

FURTHER READING

Fauchald, Nick. *William Lloyd Garrison: Abolitionist and Journalist.* Mankato, Minn.: Compass Point, 2005.

Mayer, Henry. *All on Fire: William Lloyd Garrison and the Abolition of Slavery.* New York: W.W. Norton, 2008.

Gradualism

The idea that slavery in the United States should end gradually rather than immediately. Early American **abolitionist** groups adopted the concept of gradualism, believing slavery should be phased out slowly so that the economy of the South, which depended upon slave labor, would not be disrupted. Some white abolitionists also believed that, over time, American slavery would die out on its own.

Most state **abolition** laws of the eighteenth century only stated that slaves would be freed at some future date. In 1780, Pennsylvania adopted the country's first gradual abolition law, which allowed freedom for slaves at age 19 for women and at 21 for men. Over the next 20 years, most Northern states passed similar gradualist laws, with variations on the age for the liberation of slaves. Southern abolitionists tried to make their states follow these examples, but even gradual **emancipation** laws were viewed as too radical in the South.

Quaker abolitionist Benjamin Lundy was a strong supporter of gradualism. In 1821, Lundy began publishing an abolitionist newspaper called the *Genius of Universal Eman-* *cipation.* Lundy's paper expressed his support for gradual emancipation. It also outlined his gradualist plan, which involved slaves purchasing their own freedom based upon the value of the crops they produced. Lundy assured slave owners that their farm economy would not suffer if this plan went into effect. Lundy also argued that removing African Americans from the South would end the country's great conflict over slavery.

Most abolitionists who supported gradualism, including Benjamin Lundy, viewed **colonization** as an important part of any emancipation plan. This involved freeing all African American slaves and then returning them to Africa. In 1776, Thomas Jefferson had first outlined a colonization plan for African Americans. Jefferson was a **slaveholder** who hated slavery as a concept. Yet, like many Americans, he believed that blacks were inferior to whites and could not live equally as free people in the same society. Colonization seemed like a good solution to many for the problem of slavery; African Americans would be freed, but they would not enter American society.

In 1816, the American Colonization Society was founded by a group of Presbyterian ministers. The society's goal was to encourage free blacks to **immigrate** to Africa. Some supporters of the American Colonization Society included former American presidents James Madison (1809–1817) and James Monroe (1817–1825), and Kentucky senator and slaveholder Henry Clay. In 1821, the American Colonization Society purchased a colony in West Africa, which they named Liberia, and sent thousands of freed slaves there. However, many African American abolitionists did not support the concept of colonization and instead hoped that freed slaves could become part of American society.

As a young man, abolitionist William Lloyd Garrison was a supporter of gradualism. In 1829, he joined Benjamin Lundy's *Genius of Universal Emancipation* as associate editor. Nevertheless, Garrison grew increas-ingly critical of Lundy on the issue of colonization. In 1831, he began publishing his own antislavery newspaper, *The Liberator*, which rejected both gradualism and colonization. As Garrison put it, "Gradualism in theory is perpetuity in practice."

See also: Garrison, William Lloyd; Immediatism; *Liberator, The.*

Grimke, Sarah and Angelina

See Women and the Abolitionist Movement.

H–I

Harpers Ferry

In present-day West Virginia, historic town located on a strip of land where the Potomac and Shenandoah rivers converge. The area earned its name some time after 1747, when Robert Harper purchased land there and began operating a ferry business.

After the American Revolution (1775–1783), President George Washington (1789–1797) selected the town as one of the first locations for a federal **armory** and **arsenal**, where weapons and ammunition would be made and stored. The armory and arsenal helped make Harpers Ferry a strategic point in the **abolitionist** movement and the Civil War (1861–1865). Harpers Ferry was part of Virginia until 1863, when part of that state broke away to form the new state of West Virginia.

JOHN BROWN'S RAID

John Brown, who was already an active abolitionist, became a leader of the radical abolitionist movement. On his many business trips to the East, Brown befriended several wealthy and influential abolitionists. He convinced these allies of the need for violent action and asked for money to finance his plans.

In 1855, Brown's sons settled in the Kansas Territory to oppose the proslavery government in place there. The Browns supported a rival free-state government that was formed to try to keep the Kansas Territory from being admitted to the Union as a slave state. The opposing territorial governments were involved in a series of deadly clashes. Proslavery groups initiated the violence by terrorizing and murdering antislavery settlers. Using money

HISTORY MAKERS
John Brown (1800–1859)

Born in Torrington, Connecticut, in 1800, John Brown grew up in Hudson, Ohio, where his family moved in 1805. Owen Brown instilled in John the importance of respect for all people. Unlike their neighbors, the Brown family befriended the many Native American tribes around Hudson. As a young boy, John observed the mistreatment of an African American slave owned by a family with whom he was traveling. These lessons from his youth, along with his strong religious beliefs, formed Brown's abolitionist views.

Despite his strong Christian beliefs and high moral standards, Brown's antislavery views were even stronger. As a radical abolitionist leader, he participated in the murders of several proslavery settlers in the Kansas Territory. In the Pottawatomie Massacre, Brown instigated the retaliatory murders of five proslavery men.

After the failed raid on Harpers Ferry, Brown was found guilty of treason, murder, and inciting **insurrection**. On December 2, 1859, John Brown was hanged in Charles Town, Virginia. News reports claim that the condemned abolitionist paused to kiss a small African American child on the way to his execution.

raised by his friends in the East, Brown and his sons led the antislavery forces, killing several proslavery settlers in retaliation for the attacks. Brown's leadership earned him the respect—and money—of the wealthy Easterners who funded his efforts.

After a stable government restored order to the Kansas Territory, Brown focused his attention on Harpers Ferry and its huge federal arsenal. He planned to capture the arsenal and arm the local slave population so they could aid in the revolt. Brown, his raiders, and the freed local slaves would then travel through the South, their group gaining strength by freeing and arming other slaves along the way.

Late on the night of October 16, 1859, Brown and a small group of men set their plan in motion. By the early morning hours of October 17, they had taken several hostages and seized control of the arsenal at Harpers Ferry. Unfortunately for Brown and his men, the slave uprising that he had planned never happened. Brown's plan had failed, and now he was trapped. After holding the arsenal for just over one day, Brown and his surviving men were captured.

CIVIL WAR BATTLEGROUND

Although John Brown's siege of the arsenal at Harpers Ferry failed to result in a massive slave revolt, it is widely regarded as the event that pushed the United States to civil war. The next several years saw the devastation of Harpers Ferry as it became a key battleground in the conflict.

During the early years of the Civil War, Union and Confederate troops alternately occupied Harpers Ferry. The town changed hands several times, and most of the local population fled the area. In 1863, Union forces took control of Harpers Ferry for the remainder of the war. Their presence revived the local economy and inspired many citizens to return home. Unfortunately for the local population, this renewed prosperity did not last long.

POSTWAR CHANGES

After the Civil War ended, the Union forces occupying Harpers Ferry left town. Local manufacturing declined, but Harpers Ferry maintained its prominent place in the abolitionist history of the United States. One of the nation's first racially integrated colleges, Storer College, was founded there in 1867 and remained operational well into the 1900s.

See also: Kansas-Nebraska Act.

FURTHER READING

Brackett, Virginia. *John Brown: Abolitionist.* New York: Chelsea House, 2001.

Reynolds, David S. *John Brown, Abolitionist: The Man Who Killed Slavery, Sparked the Civil War, and Seeded Civil Rights.* New York: Alfred A. Knopf, 2005.

Immediatism

The idea that slavery in the United States should end immediately. The idea became the focus of most **abolitionist** groups in the 1830s. Although many free blacks had called for an immediate end to slavery, the early abolitionist groups supported gradualism, or the phasing out of slavery over time. They were concerned that the Southern economy, which depended upon slave labor, would be harmed if slavery ended abruptly. Early abolitionists were also concerned that freed slaves would not be able to easily enter free society.

RADICAL ABOLITIONISTS

During the 1830s, however, a more radical group of abolitionists emerged, led by William Lloyd Garrison, founder of the American Anti-Slavery Society and publisher of the abolitionist newspaper *The Liberator*. Those who took the immediatist position believed that slavery was illegal and immoral, and demanded that all slaves be freed immediately.

By 1830, there were about 2 million slaves in the United States, more than double the number of slaves just 40 years earlier. Slavery was a problem that no one in the country could ignore any longer. Southerners continued to defend the institution of slavery, while antislavery societies became more vocal in their attacks against it.

In 1832, William Lloyd Garrison founded the New England Anti-Slavery Society, which was the first immediatist society in the country. The following year, Garrison helped organize the American Anti-Slavery Society. Like many early abolitionists, Garrison had at first supported **colonization**, which called for freeing African American slaves and returning them to Africa. However, by the 1830s, Garrison and his abolitionist followers had rejected colonization as a solution. They recognized that many whites had favored colonization simply because it would decrease the number of African Americans in the country. Furthermore, many African Americans considered the United States their home and did not wish to move to Africa. In 1831, a convention of free blacks meeting in New York declared, "This is our home, and this is our country. Beneath its sod lie the bones of our fathers; for it some of them fought, bled, and died. Here we were born, and here we will die."

OPPOSING COLONIZATION

In the same year that William Lloyd Garrison founded the New England Anti-Slavery Society, he also published a book called *Thoughts on African Colonization*, which attacked the idea of colonization. By including in his book quotes from members of the American Colonization Society, Garrison pointed out that many members were not only **racist** but also proslavery. He argued that most members of the society thought that colo-

nization was simply the best way to solve what they perceived to be the problem of having free blacks in American society.

In contrast to earlier abolitionist societies, which excluded African Americans from their ranks, the new immediatist societies welcomed both white and black members. Some also encouraged the participation of women. Supporters of immediatism found that the earlier approaches to ending slavery, such as political reform, were ineffectual and instead demanded total **emancipation** and equal rights for African Americans. The new abolitionist groups that embraced immediatism, especially the American Anti-Slavery Society, were ultimately the ones who most influenced the government to abolish slavery in 1865.

See also: American Anti-Slavery Society; Garrison, William Lloyd; Gradualism; Racism.

K–L

Kansas-Nebraska Act (1854)

Passed by the U.S. Congress on May 30, 1854, a **bill** that allowed the **territories** of Kansas and Nebraska to decide whether or not to permit slavery within their borders. The bill was introduced by Illinois senator Stephen A. Douglas (1847–1861). Douglas had long insisted that the best solution to the slavery issue in the United States was to allow settlers of a new territory to decide for them-

selves whether or not slavery would be permitted. This idea was known as popular sovereignty.

NEW TERRITORIES TO SETTLE

In the late 1840s and 1850s, the United States continued its expansion west. More and more Americans sought the rich farmland that made up what is now Kansas and Nebraska. In 1852, Stephen Douglas, chair of the Senate Committee on Territories, proposed that this area be opened to settlement. The area was part of the **Louisiana Territory**, a huge piece of land that stretched from the Mississippi River west to the Rocky Mountains. Until this time, the Missouri Compromise of 1820 had determined whether or not the territory would permit slavery. The Missouri Compromise declared that slavery was only permitted below the southern border of Missouri. Because the land that would become Kansas and Nebraska was above this line, slavery would not be permitted.

Two years earlier, in 1850, California had been admitted as a free state. The United States now consisted of more free states than slave states, which meant a free-state majority in the Senate. Because of its greater population, the North also had a majority in the House of Representatives. Many Southerners believed that they could prevent the North from ending slavery in the United States if they regained at least an equal balance in the Senate. If both Kansas and Nebraska became free states, Southerners feared they might never be able to regain that balance.

PASSAGE OF THE BILL

Stephen A. Douglas wrote two versions of the bill before coming up with the final Kansas-Nebraska Act. The first bill created a single territory, but a later bill allowed for the creation of the two territories of Kansas and Nebraska. Southern members of Congress demanded that a clause be added to this later bill, repealing the Missouri Compromise and allowing for slavery in Kansas. Douglas agreed,

and his final bill established the territories of Kansas and Nebraska and declared the Missouri Compromise "inoperative," which allowed the territories to decide for themselves whether to allow slavery.

Because of Douglas's influence among proslavery Northerners in the Senate and the House of Representatives, the Kansas-Nebraska Act passed in both houses. However, President Franklin Pierce (1853–1857) initially opposed it. Pierce felt that the Missouri Compromise had kept peace between the North and the South for the past 24 years and should remain in effect. Several Southern senators, however, threatened that Pierce would lose their support if he did not support the Kansas-Nebraska Act. This caused Pierce to agree to sign the bill.

Many Northerners feared that the Kansas-Nebraska Act would lead to the expansion of slavery throughout the country. The Republican Party was formed soon after the passage of the act as an opposition party, with its primary purpose to prevent the expansion of slavery in the United States. African American **abolitionist** Frederick Douglass called the bill "an open invitation to a fierce and bitter strife." Soon after the Kansas-Nebraska Act became law, violence erupted.

"BLEEDING KANSAS"

Thousands of proslavery and antislavery settlers rushed to the newly created Kansas Territory. Some of these settlers simply wanted new land, but many others came to vote in the first election either for a proslavery or antislavery government. Many **slave-holders** from Missouri were part of the rush to vote, but did not settle in Kansas. Violence soon broke out between the rival groups, with abolitionist John Brown and his sons leading the antislavery side. The territory earned the nickname "Bleeding Kansas" as the violence increased.

By the end of 1855, there were two competing governments in Kansas. The proslavery government won the popular sovereignty election through the use of illegal votes made by Missouri slaveholders who had rushed to Kansas to add their votes. Settlers who belonged to the **Free-Soil Party**, an abolitionist political party, rejected the proslavery government. Instead, they wrote their own constitution, which prohibited slavery, and established their own government in Topeka. President Pierce's administration supported the proslavery government, but Congress knew that the election was fraudulent and refused to recognize it. As a result, Kansas was not allowed to become a state. By 1859, however, antislavery settlers outnumbered proslavery settlers, and a new constitution was written. On January 29, 1861, just before the start of the Civil War (1861–1865), but after some Southern states had seceded, Kansas was finally admitted to the Union as a free state.

See also: Compromise of 1850; Congress, United States; Harpers Ferry; Lincoln-Douglas Debates; Missouri Compromise; Popular Sovereignty; Republican Party and Abolitionism.

FURTHER READING

McArthur, Debra. *The Kansas-Nebraska Act and Bleeding Kansas in American History.* Berkeley Heights, N.J.: Enslow, 2001.

The Liberator

An **abolitionist** newspaper founded by William Lloyd Garrison in 1831, *The Liberator* ran from January 1, 1831, to December 29, 1865. Garrison published weekly issues of the paper for 35 years, without missing a single issue. Its circulation was only about 3,000, and free African Americans made up most of its audience. However, *The Liberator* was known throughout the country for its unwavering stand against slavery and for Garrison's often harsh language and controversial topics.

On January 1, 1831, Garrison and his business partner Isaac Knapp published the first issue of *The Liberator* out of a small office in Boston. They were determined to print it as long as they could afford to do so. Garrison was the main writer and editor for the newspaper. He and Knapp also set the type, made copies, and mailed out the newspaper. Garrison was able to keep the paper going through donations from white abolitionists and free blacks in the Northern cities of Philadelphia, New York, and Boston.

Through *The Liberator*, William Lloyd Garrison was able to voice his views on slavery and the rights of black Americans. Garrison used his paper as a way to change the focus of the abolitionist movement from gradualism to immediatism. He attacked the gradualist American Colonization

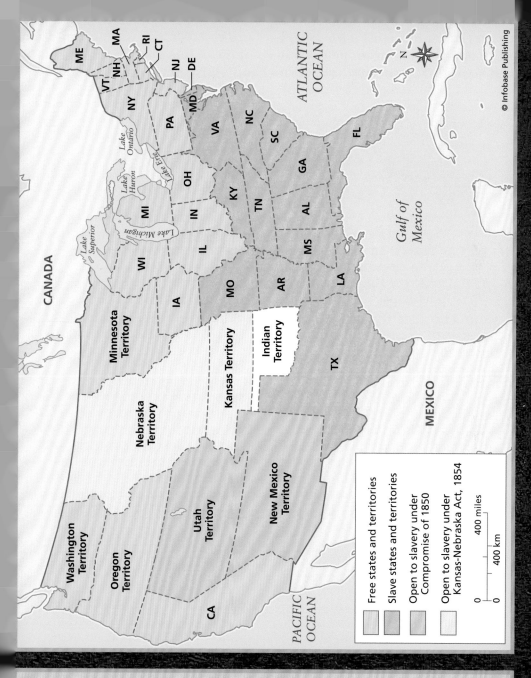

© Infobase Publishing

Map legend:

- Free states and territories
- Slave states and territories
- Open to slavery under Compromise of 1850
- Open to slavery under Kansas-Nebraska Act, 1854

0 — 400 miles
0 — 400 km

The Missouri Compromise of 1820 had attempted to limit the expansion of slavery. However, the Compromise of 1850 permitted the growth of slavery into the Utah and New Mexico territories, and the 1854 Kansas-Nebraska Act allowed the possibility of slavery's extension into the Kansas and Nebraska territories—as far north as the Canadian border.

Society, whose members believed that all African Americans should be freed from slavery and then sent to Africa. Garrison also used *The Liberator* to address important national issues and current events related to slavery, such as the Kansas-Nebraska Act of 1854 and the *Dred Scott* decision of 1857.

The Liberator was an important source of information for free blacks and those slaves who could read.

History Speaks

"To the Public"

On January 1, 1831, William Lloyd Garrison published the first copy of his abolitionist newspaper, *The Liberator*. In it he included an open letter called "To the Public," in which he spelled out the mission for his paper.

During my recent tour for the purpose of exciting the minds of the people by a series of discourses on the subject of slavery, every place that I visited gave fresh evidence of the fact, that a greater revolution in public sentiment was to be effected in the free states—*and particularly in New-England*—than at the south. I found contempt more bitter, opposition more active, detraction more relentless, prejudice more stubborn, and apathy more frozen, than among slave owners themselves. I determined, at every hazard, to lift up the standard of emancipation in the eyes of the nation, *within sight of Bunker Hill and in the birth place of liberty*. That standard is now unfurled; and long may it float, unhurt by the spoliations of time or the missiles of a desperate foe—yea, till every chain be broken, and every bondman set free! Let southern oppressors tremble—let their secret abettors tremble—let their northern apologists tremble—let all the enemies of the persecuted blacks tremble. . . .

I am aware, that many object to the severity of my language; but is there not cause for severity? I *will* be as harsh as truth, and as uncompromising as justice. On this subject, I do not wish to think, or speak, or write, with moderation. No! no! Tell a man whose house is on fire, to give a moderate alarm; tell him to moderately rescue his wife from the hand of the ravisher; tell the mother to gradually extricate her babe from the fire into which it has fallen;—but urge me not to use moderation in a cause like the present. I am in earnest—I will not equivocate—I will not excuse—I will not retreat a single inch—AND I WILL BE HEARD. . . .

Many found inspiration in its pages. Free African American and abolitionist Frederick Douglass, who later published his own abolitionist newspaper, the *North Star*, described his experience reading *The Liberator*: "The paper came, and I read it from week to week with such feelings as it would be quite idle for me to attempt to describe. The paper became my meat and drink. My soul was set all on fire. Its sympathy for my brethren in bonds—its scathing denunciations of slaveholders—its faithful exposures of slavery—and its powerful attacks upon the upholders of the institution—sent a thrill of joy through my soul, such as I had never felt before!"

Garrison made sure to send copies of *The Liberator* to newspaper editors in the South. Some reprinted sections as a warning to their readers. However, many Southern governors and senators tried to suppress the publication of *The Liberator*. Some state governments in the South even fined distributors of *The Liberator*. Many **slaveholders** mistakenly believed that Garrison supported slave rebellions and were afraid that *The Liberator* might inspire their own slaves to revolt. Garrison, however, was a **pacifist** and did not believe in violence. Yet he did write in *The Liberator* that "our slaves have the best reason to assert their rights by violent measures, inasmuch as they are more oppressed than others."

Garrison published the last issue of *The Liberator* in December 1865, after the Thirteenth Amendment to the Constitution was ratified, abolishing slavery throughout the United States. He felt it fitting to end publication now since "the object for which the *Liberator* was commenced—the extermination of chattel slavery" had been achieved.

See also: American Anti-Slavery Society; Douglass, Frederick; *Dred Scott Decision*; Garrison, William Lloyd; Gradualism; Immediatism; Kansas-Nebraska Act; *North Star*, The; Thirteenth Amendment.

FURTHER READING

Currie, Stephen. *The Liberator: Voice of the Abolitionist Movement*. Farmington Hills, Mich.: Lucent Books, 2000.

Fauchald, Nick. *William Lloyd Garrison: Abolitionist and Journalist*. Mankato, Minn.: Compass Point, 2005.

Mayer, Henry. *All on Fire: William Lloyd Garrison and the Abolition of Slavery*. New York: W.W. Norton, 2008.

Lincoln, Abraham

See Emancipation Proclamation; Lincoln-Douglas Debates.

K–L

Lincoln-Douglas Debates

A series of political debates held between Abraham Lincoln (1861–1865) and Stephen Douglas during the 1858 campaign for one of Illinois's two U.S. Senate seats. The debates were held at seven different sites throughout Illinois. For four months, Lincoln and Douglas traveled nearly 10,000 miles (16,093 km) and spoke before huge crowds of up to 15,000 people. The debates touched on some of the most important issues the country was facing at the time, including slavery and the rights of African Americans. As a result, the debates gained national attention.

Abraham Lincoln (standing) addresses the crowd during the 1858 senatorial debate against incumbent Senator Stephen A. Douglas in Charleston, Illinois. Although Lincoln lost the senatorial election, his passionate speeches against the spread of slavery made him famous across the nation.

THE CANDIDATES

Stephen Douglas, a Democrat, had been the **incumbent** senator since 1847. Douglas was nicknamed "Little Giant," because he was short but considered a political giant. As senator, Douglas had helped enact the Compromise of 1850 and had introduced a bill to Congress that became the Kansas-Nebraska Act of 1854. Both of these bills dealt with the issue of slavery in U.S. **territories**. For both, Douglas pushed his view of popular sovereignty, which meant that territories should be allowed to decide for themselves whether or not to permit slavery. Douglas believed that popular sovereignty promoted democracy and would ensure that slavery remained a state issue, not a federal one. Douglas's Kansas-Nebraska Act set off a protest movement that led to the formation of the Republican Party in 1854.

At the time of the debates, most Americans knew little about Republican candidate Abraham Lincoln. In 1846, Lincoln had been elected to the U.S. House of Representatives as a member of the **Whig Party**. He served only one term, in which he opposed the Mexican-American War (1846–1848). Lincoln publicly denounced the war, even though the war was popular in his district. Lincoln did not run again and returned home to his law practice. After the passage of the Kansas-Nebraska Act, which he strongly opposed, Lincoln reentered politics, fearing that slavery would spread to the new territories the United States had gained in the Mexican-American War.

In 1858, the Republican Party nominated Lincoln to run against Douglas for his Senate seat. Lincoln gave a now-famous speech upon accepting the Republican nomination. The speech included the phrase, "A house divided against itself cannot stand." Lincoln was referring to the United States, which was divided between free and slave states. He continued, "I believe this government cannot endure, permanently, half slave and half free. I do not expect the Union to be dissolved—I do not expect the house to fall—but I do expect it will cease to be divided." The following month, Lincoln challenged Douglas to a series of debates about the results of the Kansas-Nebraska Act and the future of slavery in the United States.

THE DEBATES

By the time the debates began on August 21, 1858, many Americans were already caught up in the issues and the candidates. Thousands of supporters traveled by train to each debate town to watch the debates firsthand. Newspaper reporters transcribed every word, and some sent transcripts or reports of the events by telegraph to the rest of the country. Though the debates were described in many reports as suspenseful, the candidates expressed many views they had already stated before.

Differing views of slavery During the debates, Lincoln and Douglas spent much of their time contrasting their views on the problem of slavery and how it should be solved. Douglas defended his stance on popular sovereignty by arguing that the problem of slavery could best be handled by state governments and not by Congress. He insisted that the Constitution had left the establishment of slavery up to individual states. Lincoln, on the other hand, pointed out that the Constitution was a document meant to extend freedom, not slavery, in the United States. He argued that, if Northerners allowed slavery to extend into the new territories, slavery would eventually become a national institution. As Lincoln pointed out in the final debate, "What has ever threatened our liberty and prosperity save and except this institution of Slavery? If this is true, how do you propose to improve the condition of things by enlarging Slavery—by spreading it out and making it bigger?"

The Dred Scott decision Lincoln also argued against the Supreme Court's *Dred Scott* decision (1857), which ruled that slaves could never be citizens of the United States and that Congress had no authority to prohibit slavery in federal territories. Lincoln expressed the fear that another Supreme Court decision could force free states to permit slavery.

During the debate in Freeport, Lincoln challenged Douglas to explain how popular sovereignty could work in light of the *Dred Scott* decision. If Congress could not legally prohibit slavery from territories, Lincoln wondered, how could settlers themselves prohibit slavery from a **territory**? Douglas explained that the settlers could do this by refusing to pass laws that would protect the property rights of **slaveholders**. Without protection, no one would bring slaves into a territory. Douglas's response was acceptable to many Northern Democrats, but it angered Southerners, and ultimately led to a division in the Democratic Party.

THE ELECTION

When the election took place in November, Stephen Douglas narrowly won the Senate seat. Despite this, Abraham Lincoln's great skill in the debates had gained him national recognition. Lincoln later referred to his defeat in the Senate race as "a slip and not a fall."

Just two years later, in 1860, Lincoln and Douglas ran against each other again, this time in the presidential election. The Lincoln-Douglas debates were printed as a book and used in the campaign. Douglas's remarks in the debates had damaged his reputation as a national leader in the Democratic Party. Lincoln easily defeated Douglas and two other candidates in the election and became the first Republican president of the United States. The following year, the divided country was swept up in a Civil War (1861–1865). On January 1, 1863, President Lincoln issued the Emancipation Proclamation, which freed the slaves in the **seceded** states that were not under Union control. It was the beginning of the end of slavery in the United States.

See also: Compromise of 1850; Congress, United States; *Dred Scott* Decision; Emancipation Proclamation; Kansas-Nebraska Act; Popular Sovereignty; Republican Party and Abolitionism; Slavery.

FURTHER READING

Bergan, Michael. *The Lincoln-Douglas Debates.* Mankato, Minn.: Compass Point, 2006.

Pierce, Alan. *The Lincoln-Douglas Debates.* Edina, Minn.: ABDO and Daughters, 2004.

M–N

Massachusetts Anti-Slavery Society

A group founded in Boston in 1832 by abolition leader William Lloyd Garrison (1805–1879). The society was founded as the New England Anti-Slavery Society and became the Massachusetts Anti-Slavery Society three years later. It was the first antislavery society to promote immediatism, or the immediate end to slavery and the immediate establishment of equal rights for African Americans.

William Lloyd Garrison wrote a constitution for the New England Anti-Slavery Society, which stated in part, "we believe that Slavery is contrary to the precepts of Christianity, dangerous to the liberties of the country, and ought immediately to be abolished; and whereas, we believe that the citizens of New-England not only have the right to protest against it, but are under the highest obligation to seek its removal by a moral influence . . ."

In its early years, the New England Anti-Slavery Society started **petition** campaigns against the slave trade and formed committees to protect the rights of free blacks. One of its most important achievements was its attacks on the American Colonization Society. Before the 1830s, the American Colonization Society was the main **abolitionist** organization among whites in the United States. Its members believed that, once slavery ended, all free African Americans should be sent to a colony in Africa. William Lloyd Garrison published a book in 1832 called *Thoughts on African Colonization*, which attacked **colonization** and argued that the American Colonization Society was actually a **racist** organization. Lecturers for the New England Anti-Slavery Society used Garrison's book in their speeches around the country. Over the next few years, most abolitionists rejected the concept of colonization.

In 1833, a group of abolitionists, including William Lloyd Garrison, Theodore Weld, Arthur Tappan, and Lewis Tappan, founded the American Anti-Slavery Society, which became the leading abolitionist society in the United States. The New England Anti-Slavery Society became a local chapter of the national society and changed its name to the Massachusetts Anti-Slavery Society in 1835.

See also: American Anti-Slavery Society; Douglass, Frederick; Garrison, William Lloyd; Gradualism; Immediatism; Racism.

FURTHER READING

Fauchald, Nick. *William Lloyd Garrison: Abolitionist and Journalist.* Mankato, Minn.: Compass Point, 2005.

Mayer, Henry. *All on Fire: William Lloyd Garrison and the Abolition of Slavery.* New York: W.W. Norton, 2008.

Mexican-American War

See Compromise of 1850.

Middle Passage

See Slavery.

Missouri Compromise (1820)

A congressional agreement that allowed for two new states to be admitted to the Union, one free and one slave, and set a boundary for the extension of slavery into new Western **territories**. In 1803, the United States had purchased the **Louisiana Territory**, a huge piece of land from France. The territory extended west from the Mississippi River all the way to the Rocky Mountains. The question about whether these new Western territories should allow slavery was a topic of great debate in both the North and South. Any new state added to the Union would tip the balance in Congress depending upon whether the territory entered as a free state or a slave state.

THE MISSOURI QUESTION

In 1818, Congress was forced to confront this issue and was challenged to come up with a solution. That year, the Missouri Territory **petitioned** Congress for admission to the Union. At the time, there were 11 free states and 11 slave states, and therefore an equal number of senators in the

M–N

Senate. Because the House of Representatives is based on individual states' populations, the greater population in the North meant that the Northern states had many more members in the House than the slave states of the South. The Missouri Territory, which already had plenty of **slaveholder** settlers, applied to enter as a slave state. If this happened, it would upset the even number in the Senate and would reduce the Northern majority in the House.

Northerners refused to allow another slave state into the Union. After a bill was sent to the House to approve Missouri's application for statehood, New York representative James Tallmadge added an amendment to the bill. The amendment stated that no new slaves could be brought into Missouri and required that any slave born there be emancipated at age 25. The bill passed in the House, with its strong Northern majority, but it did not pass in the Senate, where there were an equal number of Northerners and Southerners. Southern senators argued that Congress had no power to exclude slavery from Missouri, and they rejected the bill.

THE COMPROMISE

In 1819, Maine, then a part of Massachusetts, applied for statehood. It was clear that the South would never approve of adding another free state. Speaker of the House Henry Clay of Kentucky saw this as an opportunity for compromise. Clay was a slaveholder, but he supported the concept of gradualism, which called for the slow but steady end of slavery over an unspecified period of time. He knew, however, that the South would never agree to end slavery in Missouri, even if it was gradual. Clay felt that both sides should have to give up something or a decision would never be reached. Therefore, Clay proposed what became known as the Missouri Compromise. He recommended that Maine not be admitted to the Union as a free state unless Missouri was admitted as a slave state at the same time. This would keep the balance in the Senate.

Slavery in the territories There still remained the question of whether or not to allow slavery to extend into the rest of the Louisiana Territory. This was the most difficult issue to settle. Illinois senator Jesse Thomas added a further condition to the Missouri Compromise: all the territory north of the southern boundary of Missouri, except Missouri, would be free, and all the territory below that line could allow slavery. The compromise line was set at the 36° 30' **parallel** north.

The decision The Senate met to debate on the "Missouri Question" in January 1820. The debate was followed across the country as Northern and Southern senators made speeches either defending or attacking slavery. Ultimately, the majority of the Senate agreed to the Missouri Compromise. The balance in the Senate was maintained. Slavery would be limited in the Western territories but not completely prohibited. Part of the Missouri Compromise also stipulated that, if **fugitive** slaves escaped to the north of the compromise line, they could be caught and returned to their owners. Henry Clay also added a clause, in which Missouri had to **amend** its state constitution in order to recognize free African Americans as citizens. President James Monroe (1817–1825) signed the Missouri Compromise into law in March 1820. A great triumph for Henry Clay, he became known as The Great Compromiser.

THE END OF THE MISSOURI COMPROMISE

The following month, former president Thomas Jefferson (1801–1809) wrote to Massachusetts representative John Holmes about his response to the Missouri Compromise. He explained that the division of the country created by the compromise line worried him: ". . . this momentous question, like a fire bell in the night, awakened and filled me with terror. I considered it at once as the knell of the Union. It is hushed indeed for the moment. But this is a reprieve only, not a final sentence." John Quincy Adams, then secretary of state, wrote in his diary, "If the Union must be dissolved, slavery is precisely the question upon which it ought to break. For the present, however, this contest is laid asleep."

Both men were correct. The Missouri Compromise of 1820 was only a temporary solution, and it simply postponed the conflict over slavery in the United States. As the United States acquired more land, and new territories applied for statehood, new compromises became necessary. In 1854, when additional territories in the West applied for statehood, the Missouri Compromise was **repealed** by an act of Congress. The Kansas-Nebraska Act stated that the settlers of these territories could decide for themselves whether to allow slavery when they applied for statehood. It ignored the line that had been drawn by the Missouri Compromise. Three years later, the Supreme Court declared the Missouri Compromise unconstitutional. In the case *Dred Scott v. Sanford* (1857), the Supreme Court ruled that Congress had no authority to allow or prohibit slavery in any state. Now any state could choose to allow slavery within its borders. The "contest that had been laid to sleep" was reawakened and would soon lead to Civil War (1861–1865).

See also: Clay, Henry; Compromise of 1850; Congress, United States; *Dred Scott* Decision; Kansas-Nebraska Act.

FURTHER READING

Forbes, Robert Pierce. *The Missouri Compromise and Its Aftermath: Slavery and the Meaning of America.* Chapel Hill: University of North Carolina Press, 2007.

M–N

North Star, The

A weekly **abolitionist** newspaper founded in 1847 by free African American Frederick Douglass. The views expressed in this paper often clashed with those expressed in William Lloyd Garrison's abolitionist newspaper, *The Liberator*.

In 1838, Douglass had recently escaped from slavery and moved to Massachusetts. He came across *The Liberator* and immediately began subscribing. Three years later, Douglass met Garrison at an antislavery society meeting. Both men were greatly impressed with each other. Garrison asked Douglass to speak at the Massachusetts Anti-Slavery Society convention in Nantucket. It was Douglass's first official lecture as an abolitionist, and it became the event that sparked his career.

Douglass was a powerful speaker, and his experiences as a former slave provided his audiences with an important firsthand account of slavery. In 1845, Douglass published *Narrative of the Life of Frederick Douglass, an American Slave, Written by Himself* to prove that the stories from his life were all true. After the publication of his book, Douglass lectured in Great Britain for two years to convince the abolitionists there to join the American cause. While there, Douglass began to reconsider his thoughts about the American abolitionist movement.

AN AFRICAN AMERICAN VOICE

At first, Douglass shared William Lloyd Garrison's views, which called for the immediate, but peaceful, end to slavery in the United States. Yet Douglass grew frustrated with Garrison's views on how to go about this. The American Anti-Slavery Society, which was cofounded by Garrison, was the leading abolitionist society in the United States. Although Douglass had spoken often at its meetings, most of the other leaders were white and did not always consider the views of African American members. Douglass believed that African Americans could have a say in society once slavery was abolished only if they were leaders in the antislavery movement.

When Douglass returned to the United States in 1847, he was determined to start an African American–run newspaper that supported abolitionism. Douglass moved to Rochester, New York, to start his paper. From lectures he had given there, Douglass knew that Rochester had an active abolitionist community. Perhaps, most importantly, Rochester was a place that was not in direct competition with William Lloyd Garrison's *The Liberator*. Being in a new city gave Douglass independence from Garrison and allowed him to further develop his own ideas.

The first issue Douglass published the first issue of his paper on December 3, 1847. It was called the *North Star*, after the star in the night sky that had directed many slaves north to freedom. Douglass wanted his newspaper to "promote the moral and intellectual improvement of the colored people, and hasten the day of freedom to the three million of our enslaved fellow countrymen." Once the *North Star* entered circulation, it received praise from many abolitionists, but Rochester citizens were not happy to have their town associated with an antislavery paper, especially one edited by a former slave. Over time, however, many people in the town of Rochester grew proud of being identified with the *North Star* and Frederick Douglass.

Douglass used his paper to write freely on topics that interested him, topics that often contradicted William Lloyd Garrison's views. Garrison's views were considered radical even within the abolitionist movement. He believed that abolitionism was a moral issue and not a political one, and that the U.S. Constitution was a proslavery document. He also felt that the free states of the Union should secede and form their own country.

Douglass did not support the breakup of the United States and believed that the Constitution could be used to help the antislavery movement. He also saw politics as a useful tool for helping to advance the cause of abolitionism. Although Douglass agreed that ending slavery should be done as peacefully as possible, he supported self-defense for slaves so that they could obtain their freedom. Both Douglass and Garrison wrote about their divergent views in their newspapers, sometimes criticizing each other. Their relationship was never the same.

Later years of publication The *North Star* became well known throughout the country and was the leading African American newspaper, with a circulation of more than 4,000

in the United States and Europe. However, the cost of publishing the newspaper was high. At first, Douglass had to use his own savings and contributions from friends to keep the paper going. He also raised money for the paper by lecturing around the country.

Douglass published the *North Star* until June 1851, when it was merged with another newspaper, created by supporters of the Liberty Party, to become *Frederick Douglass's Paper*. The newspaper continued to be published as a weekly until 1860. Then it was published as *Douglass' Monthly* until it ceased being published in 1863.

See also: American Anti-Slavery Society; Garrison, William Lloyd; Slave Narratives; *Liberator, The.*

FURTHER READING

Douglass, Frederick. *Narrative of the Life of Frederick Douglass.* Clayton, Dela.: Prestwick House, 2004.

Sterngass, Jon. *Frederick Douglass.* New York: Chelsea House, 2009.

Popular Sovereignty

A political term meaning "rule by the people." The term is usually used to refer to political issues that are settled by a popular vote. During the 1850s, popular sovereignty referred to the idea that settlers of federal **territories** should decide whether or not to allow slavery in their state before they joined the Union.

The Preamble to the U.S. Constitution begins with the words "We the people." This is generally understood to mean that American citizens are governed by popular sovereignty, or rule by the people. The Framers of the Constitution based their new document on the belief that political authority resides not in the government but rather in the people themselves. Under this concept, Americans own their government but elect representatives, such as the members of Congress, to serve their interests. Ultimately, therefore, the people have the highest authority.

POPULAR SOVEREIGNTY IN CONGRESS

During the mid-nineteenth century, as many Americans debated the issue of slavery, popular sovereignty was considered to be one solution to the problem. Illinois senator Stephen A. Douglas, who strongly favored popular sovereignty, introduced the idea to Congress. Douglas believed that, to solve the problem of slavery, the issue needed to be taken out of national politics and decided on by the people of each state.

Douglas argued that popular sovereignty formed the basis of American self-government and claimed that it would "impart peace to the country and stability to the Union." Once slavery was no longer a national issue, Douglas believed that the Union would no longer be in danger of dividing into free and slave states. Douglas thought that settlers in a new territory should immediately vote on whether or not to allow slavery within its borders. Other supporters of the concept believed that the vote should take place only when the territory was prepared to **petition** for statehood.

POPULAR SOVEREIGNTY IN PRACTICE

Popular sovereignty was first used as a political strategy in the Compromise of 1850, a series of five bills that addressed various issues relating to slavery. In one bill, Congress authorized the citizens of the New Mexico Territory to decide for themselves whether to allow slavery when they applied for statehood. However, the United States outlawed slavery in 1865, and New Mexico did not apply for statehood until 1912, so popular sovereignty was never an issue there.

In 1854, popular sovereignty was again employed as a political strategy by Congress, with very different results. Two years earlier, Stephen Douglas, chair of the Senate Committee on Territories, proposed that a large area in the western United States be opened to settlement. Until this time, the terms of the Missouri Compromise had been used to determine the status of slavery in new territories. The Missouri Compromise had established a boundary that permitted slavery only below the southern border of Missouri. According to the compromise, the new territory in question could not allow slavery. Nevertheless, Southern senators refused to approve any bill that allowed another free state to enter the Union. To address this issue, Douglas wrote a bill called the Kansas-Nebraska Act. This bill established the new territories of Kansas and Nebraska, and it authorized settlers there to use popular sovereignty to decide for themselves whether or not to allow slavery. The act was passed by Congress.

After the passage of the Kansas-Nebraska Act, thousands of proslavery and antislavery settlers rushed to the newly created Kansas Territory, each side creating their own territorial government. Violence soon erupted between them, giving the new territory the nickname of "Bleeding Kansas." Kansas was not admitted to the Union until 1861, seven years later, as a free state. The violence in Kansas made it clear to most Americans that popular sovereignty was not a good solution to the problem of slavery.

See also: Compromise of 1850; Congress, United States; Kansas-Nebraska Act; Lincoln-Douglas Debates; Slavery.

Quakers

People who belong to a Christian religious denomination known as the Religious Society of Friends. Members of the group are called Quakers or Friends. The Society of Friends was founded in northern England the late 1640s by people who had broken away from the mainstream Christian church. The Quakers suffered religious **persecution** in England, which sometimes resulted in arrests and even death. In the late 1600s, groups of Quakers fled to the 13 American colonies in search of religious freedom.

In 1681, Quaker William Penn (1644–1718) established the colony of Pennsylvania, which allowed religious freedom for everyone. During the eighteenth century, Quaker groups moved to the southern colonies of Virginia, Maryland, Georgia, and the Carolinas. Quakers noted that slavery went against their beliefs. They were often very active in supporting the rights of African Americans and in helping escaped slaves.

QUAKERS IN THE ABOLITIONIST MOVEMENT

Beginning in the late 1600s, Quakers were the first organized group to denounce slavery in the American colonies. The Quakers viewed slavery as a kind of war, which went against their beliefs. During meetings of the Society of Friends, Pennsylvania Quakers denounced the idea of owning slaves and encouraged members to free their slaves. Eventually, they banned slaveholding members from attending meetings.

Two important Quaker **abolitionist** leaders in the late 1700s were John Woolman and Anthony Benezet from Pennsylvania. At the time, even though few Quakers owned slaves, many were merchants who were active in the slave trade. Woolman and Benezet demanded that Quakers completely cut ties with the slave trade. They believed that, if the slave trade was stopped, slavery would eventually end. Their influence spread to many Quaker communities in the North.

In 1775, Pennsylvania Quakers established the Society for the Relief of Free Negroes, Unlawfully Held in Bondage, which was later renamed the Pennsylvania Abolition Society. It was the first abolitionist society in the United States. The Pennsylvania Abolition Society worked not only to end slavery but also to promote education and employment for free African Americans in Philadelphia.

Because of their antislavery stance, many Quakers also became involved with the Underground Railroad, a network of safe houses and

A 1790 painting by an unknown artist shows Quakers at a meeting. The Quakers do not have a clergy but meet to worship God. Since the group was organized in the late 1640s by English dissenter George Fox, the Quakers have promoted the abolition of slavery, fair treatment of Native Americans, and equality for women, among other social issues.

hiding places for runaway slaves fleeing the South. A well-known Quaker abolitionist was Thomas Garrett (1789–1871), a wealthy iron merchant whose house in Delaware was a known stop on the Underground Railroad. It is estimated that Garrett helped about 2,700 runaway slaves to freedom.

Quaker merchant Levi Coffin (1798–1877) was also an important abolitionist associated with the Underground Railroad. Coffin began to help runaway slaves when he was still a teenager in North Carolina. In 1826, Coffin moved to the town of Newport, Indiana, a free state, to set up a business. For the next 20 years, Coffin's home was a stop on the Underground Railroad, where slaves were hidden on their way to Canada. In 1847, Coffin moved to Cincinnati,

Ohio, and opened a warehouse that sold goods made only by free African Americans. In Cincinnati, Coffin continued to help slaves on the Underground Railroad. In honor of his efforts, Coffin was sometimes referred to as the "President of the Underground Railroad."

After the Civil War (1861–1865) and the freeing of the slaves, Quakers still played an important role in promoting the rights of African Americans. During the 1950s and 1960s, Quakers were active in the **civil rights movement**. Today, Quakers continue to work for the rights of various groups throughout the world.

See also: Garrett, Thomas; Gradualism; Underground Railroad.

FURTHER READING

Yount, David. *How the Quakers Invented America.* Lanham, Md.: Rowman & Littlefield, 2007.

Racism

The belief that one genetically-related group of people is superior or inferior to another. The most obvious expression of racism is slavery, particularly the enslavement of Africans in the United States. The practice of slavery was based upon the **racist** belief that Africans were inferior to European whites.

The concept of racism often has been based on the idea that there are biological differences among human groups. However, although different physical traits (such as skin color and facial features) may seem significant, there is very little genetic difference between any one human being and another. When people talk about different "races," they often are usually referring instead to groups of people with very different *cultures*—histories, customs, languages. Racism occurs when one group **discriminates** against another. For hundreds of years, throughout the world, skin color has been the basis for racist attitudes and actions.

Racism in the United States was based originally on a long-standing belief in Europe that Africans, as well as Native Americans, were separate and inferior races. During the fifteenth and sixteenth centuries, many Europeans associated "whiteness" with purity. They believed that black was the color of the devil, and therefore they associated the dark skins of Africans with evil. Because Africans were less technologically advanced than Europeans, they were often viewed as inferior. This view formed the irrational thinking on which slavery was based. When a group of people oppresses another group, the oppressors often view the oppressed people as "less than human" and therefore less deserving of human rights. Because many Europeans viewed Africans in racist terms, they used these views to justify African enslavement.

THE BEGINNINGS OF RACISM
During the fifteenth and sixteenth centuries, Europeans increasingly began to purchase slaves from Africa. The collapse of various African societies at this time led to instability throughout the region. Many societies turned to slavery as an attempt to

regain wealth. Before this time, however, slavery was rarely based on race. Most ancient cultures did not have a concept of racial purity and did not have distinctions for people of different races. In addition, slaves in ancient times were often not even considered the lowest class of people. Many worked as farmers and household servants, but some owned property and were wealthy. Also, once slaves were freed, they were rarely identified with their previous status as a slave. For most ancient cultures, slaves were more a symbol of wealth and power as opposed to an economic necessity. However, by the eighteenth century, Africans began to become associated with the most difficult and degrading forms of labor. By then, racism had provided the justification for slavery.

Racism in the Americas The English and Dutch who first settled in the American colonies in the 1600s brought their racist beliefs with them. Native Americans, whose skins were darker and whose customs were unlike those of Europeans, were viewed as "savages." Some were captured and forced into slavery.

When Africans were first brought to the colonies, some worked as **indentured servants**, as did many white Europeans. This was in fact how many Europeans paid for their trip to the American colonies. Indentured servants worked for a family for a time, usually seven to 14 years, and then were freed after their term of service ended. Indentured servants did most of the same work as slaves, but they were not bound to serve for life.

Slave codes By the early 1700s, however, Africans began to be identified solely with slavery. In 1705, Virginia became the first colony to pass what were known as slave codes, laws that all colonists were required to follow. Slave codes were designed to maintain order in the colonies based upon racism. Until this time, Africans living in the American colonies could be free or enslaved. However, slave codes clearly defined the status of Africans as slaves only. They declared that, "All servants imported and brought into the Country ... who were not Christians in their native Country ... shall be accounted and be slaves. All Negro, mulatto and Indian slaves within this dominion ... shall be held to be real estate." Slave codes denied slaves of basic human rights, defined them as property, and made them associated with the most brutal work. Slave codes also made it legal for masters to kill their slaves for disobeying them.

At the same time, slave codes elevated the status of white indentured servants. Any white person was, by virtue of being white, considered a higher class than any African American. Slave codes provided indentured servants with the same basic rights that were denied to slaves. Slave codes also made slavery a permanent condition. Now a person could be born into slavery simply by being the child of a slave. Slave codes included sections that addressed the rights of free blacks, who were still restricted in where they could live and work. Yet from this point on, being black was generally associated with slavery.

THE ABOLITIONIST MOVEMENT AND RACISM

During the American Revolution (1775–1783), many colonists in the North began to see that slavery contradicted their fight for freedom and independence. Many Northerners freed their slaves during the war, and by the late 1700s, most Northern states had passed **emancipation** laws. However, those Northerners who opposed slavery did not necessarily feel that African Americans were worthy of equal rights. Many still held the racist belief that Africans were inferior. Therefore, though they believed slavery was wrong, they did not think that African Americans should become part of American society once they were freed.

The early antislavery movement In the early **abolitionist** movement of the late 1700s and early 1800s, antislavery societies proposed the concept of gradualism, which meant that slavery should end gradually so that African Americans could learn how to integrate into society, through education and other means. However, many supporters of gradualism believed that African Americans could never be fully integrated into society. They felt that a good solution to the problem of slavery was **colonization**. Once African Americans were freed, they would be transported to a colony in Africa.

Rejecting gradualism By the 1830s, abolitionist and publisher William Lloyd Garrison became a leader in the antislavery movement. He rejected gradualism and colonization as racist, pointing out that supporters of colonization only pretended to be concerned for the rights of freed African Americans, who for the most part did not want to leave the United States for an unknown colony in Africa.

Immediatism Garrison instead demanded immediatism, or the immediate end to slavery and equal rights for African Americans. Yet Garrison's views, which also included equal rights for women, were viewed as extremely radical, even within the abolitionist movement. Many Americans believed that slavery was evil and should be abolished, but that African Americans did not deserve the same rights as whites.

RACISM AFTER THE CIVIL WAR

During Reconstruction (1865–1877), the period immediately after the Civil War, African Americans gained a number of important rights, including the right for African American men to vote and the right of American citizenship. However, once Reconstruction ended in 1877, many Southern states began to pass laws that discriminated against blacks. These new laws became known as Jim Crow laws. The name *Jim Crow* came from an African American character played by whites in minstrel shows, traveling acts that often made fun of black Americans. Jim Crow referred to the racist belief, common among many whites, that African Americans were inferior. Many of the Jim Crow laws denied African Americans the very rights they had gained during Reconstruction, including the right to vote.

Because of Jim Crow laws, some Southern states also kept African Americans and whites separate in public places. This was based upon the belief that different races should not interact together. On trains, blacks often had to sit in a special car called "The Jim Crow car." In the 1890s, an important case, *Plessy v. Ferguson* (1896), was argued in front of the U.S. Supreme Court. The Court ruled that segregation did not violate the Constitution. It said that, if services were equal for African Americans and whites, they could be separate. The *Plessy* case had a huge impact in the South. Now it was legal

A 1938 photograph shows a drinking fountain to be used by the "colored" residents of Halifax, North Carolina. Although slavery was abolished by the Thirteenth Amendment in 1865, African Americans did not achieve social equality then. In 1896, the U.S. Supreme Court ruled in *Plessy v. Ferguson* that "separate but equal" facilities—including drinking fountains, schools, theaters, and hotels—were legal. In reality, however, the facilities for blacks were never equal to those reserved for whites. The doctrine of "separate but equal" was finally struck down by the Supreme Court in *Brown v. Board of Education* (1954), which ruled that "separate facilities are inherently unequal."

to have "separate" services for African Americans and whites as long as they were "equal." This idea of "separate but equal" institutions spread to cover most public places where African Americans and whites could meet, including restaurants, theaters, public schools, and public transportation. By the early 1900s, every state in the South had passed **segregation** laws. Most of these laws lasted until the 1950s, when the civil rights movement began.

The United States no longer has laws that support segregation and discrimination against African Americans. Today, there are many laws that prevent such things. Yet racism still exists. Some Americans maintain negative stereotypes and attitudes toward African Americans and other ethnic and minority groups. In addition, racist organizations in the United States still believe that whites are superior to others. Until racist beliefs are entirely eradicated, there will never be true equality in the United States.

In November 2008, however, the people of the United States elected Barack Obama as the 44th president. He became the first African American to serve in the nation's highest office. After taking office on January 20, 2009, President Obama (2009–) reminded all Americans of their unity as a nation:

In reaffirming the greatness of our nation, we understand that greatness is never a given. It must be earned. Our journey has never been one of shortcuts or settling for less.

It has not been the path for the faint-hearted, for those who prefer leisure over work, or seek only the pleasures of riches and fame.

Rather, it has been the risk-takers, the doers, the makers of things—some celebrated, but more often men and women obscure in their labor—who have carried us up the long, rugged path towards prosperity and freedom.

For us, they packed up their few worldly possessions and traveled across oceans in search of a new life. For us, they toiled in sweatshops and settled the West, endured the lash of the whip and plowed the hard earth.

For us, they fought and died in places Concord and Gettysburg; Normandy and Khe Sanh.

Time and again these men and women struggled and sacrificed and worked till their hands were raw so that we might live a better life. They saw America as bigger than the sum of our individual ambitions; greater than all the differences of birth or wealth or faction.

See also: Emancipation Proclamation; Garrison, William Lloyd; Gradualism; Immediatism; Lincoln-Douglas Debates; Slavery.

P–R

FURTHER READING
Friedman, Laurie. *Introducing Issues with Opposing Viewpoints—Racism.* Farmington Hills, Mich.: Greenhaven Press, 2006.
Sheftel-Gomes, Nasoan. *Everything You Need to Know About Racism: An Introduction for Teens.* New York: Rosen, 2000.

Republican Party and Abolitionism

One of two major political parties in the United States and its role in ending slavery. The Republican Party was founded in 1854, partly in opposition to the Kansas-Nebraska Act, which allowed for the expansion of slavery into free Western **territories** of the United States. The Missouri Compromise of 1820 had established a boundary line for slavery in the territories, and the Kansas-Nebraska Act eliminated that line. The Kansas-Nebraska Act allowed for popular sovereignty in the territories, permitting settlers there to decide for themselves whether or not to let slavery exist.

Soon after the passage of the Kansas-Nebraska Act, meetings were held across the Midwest to discuss the formation of a new political party. One meeting in Wisconsin in March 1854 is generally considered the first meeting of the Republican Party. The Republican Party was made up of many **abolitionists**, as well as members from the former **Know-Nothing Party**, **Whig Party**, and **Free-Soil Party**. Antislavery Democrats in the North and West also joined the Republican Party. The new party was opposed to the expansion of slavery. Southern Democrats believed that Congress had no constitutional right to prohibit slavery in the territories, but the Republican Party believed that Congress had the right and ought to utilize it.

In 1856, Western explorer John C. Fremont (1813–1890) ran as the first Republican candidate for president. He won about one-third of the popular vote, losing the election to Democrat James Buchanan (1857–1861). Fremont received less than one percent of the popular vote in the South, but he won the majority of the popular vote in 11 out of the 16 Northern states.

Four years later, the Republican Party nominated Abraham Lincoln for president. Lincoln, a former Whig, had joined the Republican Party because of his opposition to the Kansas-Nebraska Act. In 1858, Lincoln had lost the race for U.S. Senate in Illinois to Stephen Douglas, who was the main author of the Kansas-Nebraska Act. Yet, during a series of debates for the Senate seat, Lincoln's powerful antislavery speeches brought him national recognition.

During the 1860 election, most of the slave states in the South threatened to **secede** from the Union if the Republicans won the presidency. In November, however, Abraham Lincoln was elected president (1861–1865). Six weeks later, South Carolina became the first Southern state to secede from the Union. By April 1861, the Civil War (1861–1865) had begun, and the issue of slavery would finally be settled.

See also: Congress, United States; Kansas-Nebraska Act; Lincoln-Douglas Debates; Missouri Compromise; Popular Sovereignty.

FURTHER READING

Schulman, Bruce J., ed. *Student's Guide to Congress.* Washington, D.C.: CQ Press, 2009.

Wagner, Heather Lehr. *The History of the Republican Party.* New York: Chelsea House, 2007.

S-T

Slave Narratives

Personal accounts of African Americans who had escaped from slavery. About 65 slave stories, or **narratives**, were published as books or pamphlets before 1865. They provided readers with a closer look at slavery. These stories contrasted greatly with **slaveholders'** descriptions of slavery, which had been used to defend slavery as an institution.

WIDESPREAD READING

Slave narratives were very popular, and many sold in the tens of thousands of copies. They were advertised in **abolitionist** newspapers and sold at abolitionist meetings, but their popularity had more to do with the fact that many were very dramatic and thrilling to read. Most slave narratives were modeled on the romantic literature of the day, which was full of drama and suspense. The stories told of the horrors of slavery, including the brutality of beatings and the harsh living conditions slaves endured. The stories described families being torn apart, children taken away from their parents—an especially moving formula in an age when the nuclear family was emerging as an institution to be both celebrated and romanticized. Readers became caught up in tales of thrilling escape and bravery. Through these narratives, slaves were portrayed as sympathetic and interesting.

STRUGGLES FOR FREEDOM

Most slave narratives followed the story of a person's journey from enslavement to freedom. The highpoint of the story was usually the former slave's final escape and arrival on free land. Slave narratives also described what slave communities were like and how slaves were able to create a unique African American culture through music, folktales, and religion. This was a world that few whites even knew existed. Some slave narratives ended with a pledge to end slavery and tried to convince readers to support the cause of abolitionism. The narratives were considered vital to the abolitionist movement because they were real documentations, personal proofs, of the many horrors of slavery.

Because slave narratives were used as persuasive documents by abolitionists, many readers questioned the authenticity of the details. Some even wondered if African Americans were really capable of writing. Because of this, many slave narratives included documentation to prove that the events described were factual. Many titles included the phrase "Written by Himself (or Herself)" for further proof.

POPULAR SLAVE NARRATIVES

The most popular slave narrative was the *Narrative of the Life of Frederick Douglass, an American Slave, Written by Himself,* published in 1845. Frederick Douglass (1818–1895) had escaped from slavery in 1838 and had become a leader in the abolitionist movement. Because Douglass had escaped, he was careful not to give away too many details of his background during his abolitionist speeches. Yet many who saw him speak could not believe that this brilliant, eloquent man was a former slave. Douglass published his narrative, including real names and details, to prove his story was true. The narrative included an introduction by white abolitionist leader William Lloyd Garrison (1805–1879), attesting to the truth of Douglass's story and praising Douglass for his work. The book became a best seller and was translated into French and Dutch and sold all over Europe.

In 1847, African American abolitionist William Wells Brown (1814–1884) published his autobiography entitled *Narrative of William W. Brown, a Fugitive Slave, Written by Himself.* Brown had escaped slavery in 1834 and gone to work for the Underground Railroad, a secret network of safe houses that had station masters who helped runaway slaves reach the North. Brown's book became the second most popular slave narrative after Douglass's.

Harriet Jacobs's (1813–1897) *Incidents in the Life of a Slave Girl,* published in 1861, was the first slave narrative written by a woman. Jacobs wrote her book under the pen name Linda Grist. The book told in very honest detail what it was like to be a female slave, and it described the hardships that enslaved women had to endure. Jacobs's story had originally been published in serial form in the *New York Tribune* but was found to be too shocking for many readers and was turned into a book.

Some former slaves wrote their narratives themselves. However, many could not read or write and had to dictate their stories, often to white abolitionists. Sojourner Truth had escaped from slavery in 1826 and had become an abolitionist speaker. In 1861, she dictated her memoirs to a friend, and it became a popular slave narrative.

Narratives by former slaves continued to be published during and after the Civil War (1861–1865). Today, they remain a valuable resource for learning about the institution of slavery.

See also: Douglass, Frederick; Garrison, William Lloyd; Slavery; Truth, Sojourner; *Uncle Tom's Cabin.*

FURTHER READING

Douglass, Frederick. *The Narrative of the Life of Frederick Douglass, An American Slave, Written by Himself.* New York: Barnes and Nobles Classics, 2005.

Drew, Benjamin. *Refugees from Slavery: Autobiographies of Fugitive Slaves in Canada.* Pecos, N.Mex.: Dover Publications, 2004.

Slavery

A system in which people are owned by others and in which those enslaved do not have the freedom to leave. Slavery has existed in some form or another throughout most of human history, in almost all cultures. The institution of slavery can be traced to the earliest written records. For example, the Code of Hammurabi, the code of laws of the ancient kingdom of Mesopotamia, written around 1780 B.C., includes laws that addressed slavery.

A slave was generally considered a person owned as "property" by someone else; the enslaved person usually had no rights or freedoms. Slaves were often kidnapped or captured in wars, but in many ancient cultures, people were sold into slavery as punishment for a crime or to pay back debts. Some slaves were of different nationalities, religions, or races than their captors, but many were the same. In the ancient world, slavery was not always a permanent condition. In many societies, slaves could become citizens after a period of time. For many families, owning slaves symbolized wealth and power and was not a necessary source of labor.

The Atlantic slave trade, which began in the fifteenth century, introduced a new kind of slavery—permanent and inherited—to the world. This cruel slave trade was part of a system of international trade between and among Europe, Africa, North America, and South America. European traders exported manufactured goods to the west coast of Africa, where they would be exchanged for slaves. The slaves were then sold in North and South America. In the Americas, traders bought raw materials such as sugar, cotton, and tobacco and shipped them back to Europe.

Between 1450 and 1850, about 12 million Africans were transported across the Atlantic Ocean to the Americas. Of these, around 600,000 Africans were sent to North America. Most others were transported to Brazil or to islands in the Caribbean. Yet, by the nineteenth century, the majority of all slaves in the Americas lived in the United States. The enslaved population there had increased mostly because of the birthrate, not the slave trade.

FROM AFRICA TO THE AMERICAS

Most slaves who were sold to Europeans in the Atlantic slave trade had been either captured in war or were enslaved as punishment for crimes or as repayment for a debt. Because of the European demand for slaves in the sixteenth century, increasing numbers of Africans were enslaved by rival groups or as punishment for minor crimes. Professional slave traders from various European countries, including England, France, Holland, and Portugal, set up slave-trading posts along the coast of West Africa.

Once Africans were captured from their villages to be sold as slaves, they were bound together and marched to the Atlantic coast, a distance that could be hundreds of miles long. As many as half of the people on these forced marches died on the way. Those who reached the coast were put into underground cells, sometimes for months. Once they were sold, slaves were chained together and forced onto ships. The journey to North and South America and the Caribbean became known as the Middle Passage, referring to the second leg of a slave ship's trip from Europe to Africa, then to the Americas, and back to Europe again.

The Middle Passage usually took about seven weeks, during which thousands more slaves died. In order to fit as many Africans as possible onto the ships, Africans were crammed in as tightly as possible, with little air to breathe and no room to stand. During the voyage, slaves were usually fed only once a day, and water was scarce. Formerly enslaved antislavery activist Olaudah Equiano (c. 1745–1797) described the Middle Passage in his autobiography: "The closeness of the place, and the heat of the climate, added to the number in the ship, which was so crowded that each had scarcely room to turn himself, almost suffocated us. . . . the air soon became unfit for respiration . . . and brought on a sickness among the slaves, of which many died." Some slaves jumped overboard in order to escape the horrifying conditions. Once the ships arrived in the Americas, most Africans were sold several times before reaching their final destination.

FROM SERVANT TO SLAVE

Before the late 1600s, the number of slaves that reached what is now the United States was very small because the institution of slavery grew slowly in America. In the early 1600s, American colonists mostly used **indentured servants** for labor. Many Europeans became indentured servants simply to pay the price of their passage to the colonies. Once there, indentured servants worked for a period of time, usually 7 to 14 years, and then were given their freedom.

In 1640, however, John Punch, a runaway black indentured servant, was sentenced to servitude for life. Punch was the first documented slave in the American colonies. As English settlers faced a shortage of white indentured servants in the late 1600s, however, they began to import thousands of slaves directly from Africa.

By the early 1700s, new laws called slave codes clearly defined the status of Africans as slaves. In 1705, Virginia became the first colony to pass slave codes. They declared that, "All servants imported and brought into the Country . . . who were not Christians in their native Country . . . shall be accounted and be slaves. All Negro, mulatto, and Indian slaves within this dominion . . . shall be held to be real estate." In addition, slave owners could legally punish and even kill slaves. According to slave codes, if a slave was killed, "the master shall be free of all punishment . . . as if such an accident never happened." Over the next few years, all the colonies had passed their own versions of slave codes.

When the American Revolution (1775–1783) began in 1775, both the British and the colonists tried to recruit slaves to serve on their side in the war. Many slaves were promised freedom if they became soldiers. During the war, many colonists in the North also freed their slaves. Thousands of others escaped to freedom. By the early 1800s, every Northern state had abolished slavery either by court decisions or by a plan of gradual **emancipation**. In the South, however, slavery continued to grow as the economic need for labor increased. Slavery was by then considered a normal part of Southern life.

LIFE UNDER SLAVERY

Most slave labor in the South was used for planting, cultivating, and harvesting single crops on **plantations**. These crops included cotton, rice, and tobacco. On the largest plantations, which were like small villages, some slaves also worked as carpenters, blacksmiths, cabinetmakers, and bricklayers. Others worked in the owners' home as cooks, maids, and weavers. Field slaves typically worked 10 hours a day, six days a week, with only Sundays off. The hardest work came during planting and harvesting times, when they were forced to work 15 hours a day or more. Children as young as three or four were put to work, doing such tasks as weeding the fields, carrying water, feeding livestock, and helping in the kitchen.

For most **slaveholders**, the hardest task was forcing slaves to work. Many slaveholders used harsh punishments, such as whipping, to control slaves. Chains and shackles were often used to keep slaves from running away. On the other hand, some slaveholders attempted to use positive reinforcements to make slaves more productive, such as gifts of food or money at the end of the year or special days off, but in the end, all slaves were not free and were forced to work against their will.

Slave Families Slave marriages and families were not recognized by American law. This meant that slave owners could break up families as they wished. It was common to split up marriages and to sell children separately from their parents. Yet despite this, many African Americans were able to maintain a large extended family network. If parents and children were sold to different plantations, grandparents, or aunts and uncles stepped in and cared for the children. Even strangers brought up children if parents were unable to take care of them.

Surviving the Harsh Reality African Americans found many ways to survive the brutality of slavery. Some showed resistance to their masters by breaking tools, pretending to be sick, or working as slowly as they could. Running away was another form of resistance. Most slaves ran away only short distances to visit family members or friends. However, some tried to escape slavery permanently, often traveling by way of the Underground Railroad. The Underground Railroad was a system of safe houses and hiding places that helped runaway slaves escape to freedom. In addition to their acts of resistance, many African Americans relied on religious and cultural traditions to help them get through the harshness of their daily lives. Many brought with them songs and stories from Africa, passing down proverbs, legends, and folklore from generation to generation.

During the early 1800s, slave ownership in the South became more concentrated. The actual number of Southerners who owned slaves began to decline. Still, most Southerners clung to their way of life and the right to own slaves. Yet at the same time, the **abolitionist** movement, which demanded the end of slavery in the United States, began to grow.

See also: American Anti-Slavery Society; Douglass, Frederick; Garrison, William Lloyd; Gradualism; Immediatism; Quakers; Thirteenth Amendment; Underground Railroad.

Slavery Today

Although slavery is outlawed in most countries today, it is practiced secretly in many parts of the world. It is estimated that there are 27 million enslaved people around the world. Slavery today is most commonly found in parts of Africa, the Middle East, and South Asia, but it is less obvious than it once was, which makes it harder to identify.

The most widely practiced form of slavery in the world is known as bonded labor. Most common in very poor areas, bonded labor exists when people or their children are forced to work for someone until they pay off a debt. Another kind of slavery is chattel slavery, which is similar to the slavery that existed in early America, in which people become the property of others and work for no money. Sex slavery occurs when women and children are forced into **prostitution**. They are either kidnapped from their homes or are tricked into the work in order to pay off debts. Forced labor is another kind of slavery. This happens when people are lured to a new place by the promise of a good job but instead find themselves working without pay. Victims of forced labor can include domestic workers and migrant workers. Thus, the evils of slavery continue today, though perhaps under different names.

FURTHER READING

Douglass, Frederick. *The Narrative of the Life of Frederick Douglass, An American Slave, Written by Himself.* New York: Barnes and Nobles Classics, 2005.

Drew, Benjamin. *Refugees from Slavery: Autobiographies of Fugitive Slaves in Canada.* Pecos, N.Mex.: Dover Publications, 2004.

Fradin, Dennis Brindell. *Bound for the North Star: True Stories of Fugitive Slaves.* New York: Clarion Books, 2000.

Slave's Friend, The

A monthly pamphlet published by the American Anti-Slavery Society, which consisted of **abolitionist** poems, songs, and stories for children. Each 16-page issue featured about a dozen short stories and poems, illustrated with small woodcuts. The illustrations included portrayals of Africans, African American slaves, and freed blacks, and many were used in more than one issue. The pamphlet cost a penny so that it would be affordable to most people. Few copies were actually sold, but many were mailed out or scattered throughout public places. In total, 38 issues were published between 1836 and 1839.

The Slave's Friend appealed to its young readers to embrace the abolitionist movement. Many stories discussed the cruelties of slavery. Some stories and poems described the lives of African children so that white children could see their humanity and recognize the suffering of enslaved African Americans. On the back cover of the first issue was printed the following: "*The Slave's Friend* is printed for children. The editor wants to have them love the poor slaves. He has tried to write this little book so that very young children can understand it. It is hoped that all the little boys and girls in the land may read it." Many abolitionists believed that children could join the fight against slavery. Children were repeatedly told that they could make a difference. They were even encouraged to collect money for the abolitionist cause. In 1837, one issue of *The Slave's Friend* was written as a guide to setting up children's antislavery societies.

Abolitionists hoped children's literature could influence American society by starting with its youngest members. They hoped to change children's attitudes about slavery and the way that African Americans were perceived. In its second issue, *The Slave's Friend* included an antislavery creed that children were to uphold:

> I believe that it is right to be kind to the poor slaves, to pray for them, and try to persuade slaveholders to give them their liberty; that it is right to say that slavery is a dreadful sin, and that it is very wicked to buy and sell men, women, and children. I believe that it is wicked to have hard feelings toward any colored people, to abuse them, or wish them any hurt.

The issue also contained a short play called "How Children Become Slaves," in which a mother explains to her son that African children were stolen from their homes and sold as slaves. The publishers of *The Slave's Friend* hoped stories like this would encourage young readers to empathize with tales of other children who were no different from themselves.

See also: American Anti-Slavery Society.

FURTHER READING
Jacobs, Harriet. *Incidents in the Life of a Slave Girl.* Rockville, Md.: Arc Manor, 2008.

Stowe, Harriet Beecher

See Uncle Tom's Cabin.

Sumner, Charles (1811–1874)

U.S. senator from Massachusetts. In 1848, Sumner became one of the founders of the Free-Soil Party, which was opposed to slavery. Born in Boston on January 6, 1811, Sumner attended the Boston Latin School. He began his higher education at Harvard University in 1830 and graduated from the Harvard Law School in 1833. After traveling in Europe between 1837 and 1840, he returned home to Massachusetts. In 1846, he declined the Whig nomination for election to the House of Representatives.

After losing the election to the House of Representatives in 1848, he later won a seat in the U.S. Senate in 1851 as a Free Soiler. He was re-elected as a Republican in 1857, 1863, and 1869 and served until his death in 1874.

After its founding in 1854, the Republican Party quickly gained supporters in the North. Just two years after the party formed, Republicans won a majority of seats in the House of Representatives in the 1856 elections. As a result, tensions in Congress were high. In May 1856, Senator Sumner gave a passionate speech against slavery, known as the "Crime Against Kansas," in which he criticized several proslavery senators. His speech infuriated South Carolina representative Preston S. Brooks. Two days later, Brooks beat Sumner unconscious with a cane on the Senate floor. As a result of severe injuries, Sumner was absent from the Senate until December 1859. This violent outburst shocked the nation and turned even more Northerners against the South.

See also: Republican Party and Abolitionism.

FURTHER READING

Donald, David Herbert. *Charles Sumner and the Coming of the Civil War.* Naperville, Ill.: Sourcebooks, 2009.

Taylor, Zachary (1784–1850)

The 12th president of the United States (1849–1850). Although a Southerner and a **slaveholder** himself, Taylor was committed to preserving the Union. During the tensions before the passage of the Compromise of 1850, Taylor threatened to call all American troops, if necessary, to end any talk of **secession**.

Zachary Taylor was born in Virginia in 1784. Soon after his birth, his family moved to a **plantation** in Kentucky, where they grew wealthy and influential. In 1808, he joined the U.S. Army and spent the next 40 years in the service.

During the War of 1812 (1812–1814), fought between the United States and Great Britain, Taylor became known for his skills as a military commander. Later, he earned the nickname "Old Rough and Ready." In 1840, Taylor was sent to Louisiana, to command the Southwest Department of the Army. He also purchased a plantation in Mississippi, where he eventually owned more than 100 slaves and became one of the most prominent plantation owners in the South.

In 1845, the Republic of Texas, which had **seceded** from Mexico in 1836, became the 28th state of the United States. However, Mexico and the United States disputed what constituted Texas's border. Unable to settle the issue peacefully, President James K. Polk (1845–1849) ordered Zachary Taylor, now a general, and his troops to go to the area of dispute. This started what became the Mexican-American War (1846–1848). Taylor became a national hero in the final battle of the war, the Battle of Buena Vista. As part of a peace treaty, Mexico handed over a large territory to the United States, which included present-day California, Nevada, Utah, and parts of Arizona, New Mexico, and Colorado.

In 1848, the **Whig Party** nominated Zachary Taylor for president. Southerners hoped that, as a slaveholder, Taylor would support the expansion of slavery into the new territories that the United States had won from Mexico. Because Northern Whigs opposed nominating a slaveholder, New York **comptroller** Millard Fillmore was added as Taylor's running mate. In a close election, Taylor won the presidency.

The question of allowing slavery into the new territories became a national debate. Despite being a slaveholder, Taylor believed that slavery was an economic necessity only in states that grew cotton. He did not believe it should extend into the new Western territories. He urged California and New Mexico to apply for statehood before the question of slavery was even addressed. Yet if both applied as free states, the free-state/slave-state balance in the U.S. Senate would become a free-state majority. Some Southerners threatened to secede from the United States if this happened. Taylor was a strong defender of the Union and threatened to hold the country together by armed force if necessary.

Members of Congress, including Henry Clay and Stephen Douglas, worked on a compromise that would allow California to enter as a free state and other territories to decide for themselves whether or not to permit slavery. To appease Southerners, the compromise also included a Fugitive Slave Law, which required escaped slaves anywhere in the country to be returned to their owners. Taylor refused to accept these terms, and it appeared that no compromise could be reached. On July 4, 1850, however, Taylor suddenly became ill and died five days later. Vice President Millard Fillmore, who supported the compromise, became president (1850–1853). The Compromise of 1850 was passed two months later and held the country together for another 10 years.

See also: Clay, Henry; Compromise of 1850; Congress, United States; Fugitive Slave Law.

FURTHER READING
Eisenhower, John S. D. *Zachary Taylor.* New York: Times Books, 2008.
Roberts, Jeremy. *Zachary Taylor.* Minneapolis, Minn.: Lerner Publications, 2008.

Thirteenth Amendment

Added in 1865 to the U.S. Constitution, it abolished slavery as a legal institution. President Abraham Lincoln (1861–1865) signed the Emancipation Proclamation on January 1, 1863, in the midst of the Civil War (1861–1865). It freed all slaves in areas of the Confederacy not under Union control. However, the Emancipation Proclamation was merely a war action that Lincoln, in his role as commander in chief, was legally allowed to make. Lincoln and many Republicans in Congress believed that an **amendment** to the Constitution was necessary so that no state or Congress could ever restore slavery.

Republican senator Lyman Trumball (1855–1873) from Illinois helped draft a proposed Thirteenth Amendment to the Constitution in March 1864. By this time, the Emancipation Proclamation had been in effect for a full year. However, there were still many Northern members of Congress opposed to a constitutional amendment that freed slaves. Some opposed it simply because they felt that winning the war would put an end to slavery and that amending the Constitution was unnecessary. In April 1864, the proposed Thirteenth Amendment was presented to the

S–T

mostly Republican Senate. It easily passed by a vote of 38 to 6. However, the required two-thirds majority needed in the House of Representatives was defeated by a vote of 93 to 65. Only four Democrats voted for it.

President Lincoln took an active role in encouraging the passage of the Thirteenth Amendment. He insisted that its passage be added to the Republican Party platform for the presidential election in November 1864.

In January 1865, the House of Representatives voted again on the Thirteenth Amendment. Every Republican in the House voted for its passage. This time, of the 199 members who finally voted for the amendment, 10 were Democrats. Their votes allowed for a two-thirds majority in the House. Indiana congressman George Julian wrote that, after the Thirteenth Amendment passed, "[m]embers joined in the shouting and kept it up for some minutes. Some embraced one another, others wept like children."

In a letter written to President Lincoln a month after the passage of the Thirteenth Amendment, **abolitionist** leader William Lloyd Garrison wrote, ". . . you have done a mighty work for the freedom of all mankind. I have the utmost faith in the benevolence of your heart, the purity of your motives, and the integrity of your spirit."

By December 18, 1865, three-fourths, or 27 of the 36 states, **ratified** the Thirteenth Amendment so that it became a part of the Constitution. Slavery had finally been prohibited in the United States.

History Speaks

The Thirteenth Amendment Abolishes Slavery

With the ratification of the Thirteenth Amendment to the U.S. Constitution in 1865, slavery was abolished throughout the states and territories. The far-reaching amendment was brief and to the point.

Section 1. Neither slavery nor involuntary servitude, except as a punishment for crime whereof the party shall have been duly convicted, shall exist within the United States, or any place subject to their jurisdiction.

Section 2. Congress shall have power to enforce this article by appropriate legislation.

See also: Emancipation Proclamation; Garrison, William Lloyd; Slavery; Congress, United States.

Truth, Sojourner (1797–1883)

African American **abolitionist** and women's rights activist whose powerful speeches moved others to join both the antislavery movement and the women's movement.

Sojourner Truth was born into slavery in 1797 on a large farm in upstate New York. She was named Isabella Baumtree, one of 13 children of James and Isabella Baumtree, who were also enslaved. Isabella was separated from her family and sold a number of times during her childhood. In 1810, she was sold to John Dumont in New Paltz, New York. While there, she married Thomas, another of Dumont's slaves, in 1817. They had five children together.

In 1799, the state of New York had planned for the gradual abolition of slavery, which would be completed on July 4, 1827. John Dumont promised Baumtree her freedom a year earlier, "if she would do well, and be faithful." Yet when the time came, Dumont denied her freedom. Infuriated, Baumtree decided to escape. One morning at dawn, she left the farm with her infant daughter, Sophia. She was forced to leave her other children behind because, by New York law, they would not be legally freed until they had worked as bound servants up until their twenties.

Baumtree walked to the home of an old friend, who directed her to the Van Wageners, a Quaker family. They took her in for about a year, when she became legally free. Once free, Baumtree worked to free her five-year-old son, Peter, who had been sold to an owner in Alabama. With the help of some Quaker abolitionists, Baumtree was able to make an official complaint in court. After months of legal dealings, Peter was returned to her. In 1829, Baumtree then moved to New York City, where she worked as a housekeeper for many years.

BECOMING SOJOURNER TRUTH

After gaining her freedom, Isabella Baumfree also became deeply religious. In 1843, at the age of 46, she changed her name to Sojourner Truth. A *sojourner* is another word for "traveler." Truth had felt a spiritual calling to become a traveling preacher. Unable to read or write, Truth became a powerful speaker. After several months of traveling, Truth's friends directed her to the Northampton Association of Education and Industry in Northampton, Massachusetts. The organization had been founded by abolitionists to support abolitionism and women's rights. The members of the Northampton Association included some of the country's most prominent abolitionists, such as William Lloyd Garrison and Frederick Douglass.

The Northampton Association disbanded in 1846 because of lack of funds. Truth remained in Northampton, buying her own home for the first time. Because Truth never learned to read or write, she dictated her memoirs to her friend Olive Gilbert. They were published by William Lloyd Garrison in 1850 as *The Narra-*

S– T

tive of Sojourner Truth: A Northern Slave. Truth's book and her legendary speeches made her a popular lecturer for both abolitionist and women's rights organizations around the country.

"AIN'T I A WOMAN?"

In 1851, Sojourner Truth attended the Ohio Women's Rights Convention in Akron. At this meeting, many men, including ministers, spoke out against women's rights. They claimed that women were weak and that men were superior. Suddenly, Truth rose from her seat. Frances Gage, a leader of the convention, described what happened next:

> "The tumult subsided at once, and every eye was fixed on this almost Amazon form, which stood nearly six feet high, head erect, and eyes piercing the upper air like one in a dream. At her first word there was a profound hush. She spoke in deep tones, which, though not loud, reached every ear in the house, and away through the throng at the doors and windows."

During her short speech, Truth described her experiences both as a former slave and a woman. She said:

> "That man over there says that women need to be helped into carriages, and lifted over ditches, and to have the best place everywhere. Nobody ever helps me into carriages, or over mud-puddles, or gives me any best place! And ain't I a woman?"

That speech is still one of the most famous women's rights speeches in American history.

After the Civil War (1861–1865), Truth worked for the National Freedman's Relief Association in Washington, D.C., which helped to improve the lives of former slaves. Truth died in 1883 at the age of 86.

See also: Douglass, Frederick; Garrison, William Lloyd; Slave Narratives; Women and the Abolitionist Movement.

FURTHER READING

Kudlinski, Kathleen V. *Sojourner Truth*. New York: Aladdin Publishing, 2003.

Truth, Sojourner. *The Narrative of Sojourner Truth*. New York: Cosimo Books, 2008.

Tubman, Harriet (c. 1820–1913)

An African American woman who was an escaped slave, **abolitionist**, and a guide on the Underground Railroad. Harriet Tubman was born into slavery around 1820 on Maryland's Eastern Shore. She was the 11th child of Benjamin and Harriet Ross, who were also slaves. Her given name was Araminta, and she was called "Minty" as a child. As an adult, however, she called herself Harriet, after her mother.

Tubman began working at the age of five when she was "loaned" to another **plantation**. By the time she was 12, she working as a field hand. Around this time, she was struck in the head by her overseer for defending another slave who had tried to run away. This injury left her with seizures for the rest of her life. In 1844, Harriet married John Tubman, a free African American. Though they were married, she was still required to continue working for her master.

ESCAPE

Harriet Tubman had always dreamed of being free, but after confiding this to her husband, he told her that if she tried running away he would turn her in. She eventually escaped in 1849, running away from the plantation with her brothers in the middle of the night. Yet her brothers were too afraid and turned back, leaving Tubman to make the journey by herself. She first found shelter in the home of a Quaker woman. Quakers actively opposed slavery, and many were part of the Underground Railroad, a secret network of safe houses that helped runaway slaves reach the North. Tubman traveled mostly at night when it was easier to hide from slave hunters. Finally, she crossed the border into the free state of Pennsylvania. She later described how she felt upon arriving: "I looked at my hands to see if I was the same person now I was free. There was such a glory over everything. The sun came like gold through the trees and over the fields, and I felt like I was in heaven."

A hand-painted photograph of Harriet Tubman shows the abolitionist leader in about 1895. Tubman escaped from slavery in 1849 and then worked to free other slaves, including her family. She also served as a Union spy during the Civil War (1861–1865).

Harriet Tubman was now free, but she was also completely alone. She decided then to help her family and friends escape from slavery as well. In Philadelphia, she found work as a cook and laundress, and saved money for her return trips. She also met William Still, a free African American who, through the Pennsylvania Anti-Slavery Society, had organized one of the most important networks of the Underground Railroad. William Still later wrote about Harriet Tubman that "a more ordinary specimen of humanity could hardly be found among the most unfortunate-looking farm hands of the South. Yet, in point of courage, shrewdness and disinterested exertions to rescue her fellow-men . . . she was without her equal."

"MOSES" OF THE UNDERGROUND RAILROAD

Harriet Tubman secretly journeyed back to Maryland about 20 times, leading slaves to freedom. Because of the Fugitive Slave Law of 1850, which required that all runaway slaves be returned to their owners, even Northern states were dangerous for escaped slaves. Thus, Tubman brought some farther north to Canada. Between 1850 and 1857, she was able to rescue her sister, her brothers, and her parents. It is estimated that she helped free about 300 slaves in total. Tubman worked closely with Quaker abolitionist Thomas Garrett (1789–1871), whose home in Wilmington, Delaware, was the last stop on the Underground Railroad before Pennsylvania. During her missions, Tubman carried a rifle with her at all times. She warned the other slaves that if they even considered turning back, they would be shot.

Tubman's bravery made her famous among abolitionists. She was also well known to **slaveholders** in the South, who offered $40,000 for her capture. However, Tubman was never caught and, as she put it, "never lost a passenger." She was often called "Moses," which referred to the biblical story in which Moses freed the Israelites from slavery in Egypt.

LATER YEARS

In 1859, Harriet Tubman bought a house for her parents from abolitionist and New York senator William H. Seward in Auburn, New York. The area was known for its active abolitionist movement, and it became an important home base for Tubman's family and friends. During the Civil War (1861–1865),) Harriet Tubman served with the Union Army as a cook, nurse, scout, and sometimes even a spy.

In addition to her abolitionist work, Harriet Tubman also believed in women's **suffrage**, or the right to vote. She attended meetings of various suffragist organizations, and in 1896, she served as a representative at the National Association of Colored Women's first annual convention. Harriet Tubman died on March 10, 1913, at the age of 93. She was given a full military funeral and was buried in Fort Hill Cemetery in Auburn, New York.

See also: Canada and the Abolitionist Movement; Fugitive Slave Law; Garrett, Thomas; Quakers; Slavery; Underground Railroad; Women and the Abolitionist Movement.

FURTHER READING

Clinton, Catherine. *Harriet Tubman: The Road to Freedom.* Boston: Back Bay Books, 2005.

Lowry, Beverly. *Harriet Tubman: Imagining a Life.* Norwell, Mass.: Anchor Press, 2008.

McDonough, Yona Zeldis. *Who Was Harriet Tubman?* New York: Grosset & Dunlap, 2002.

U–W

Uncle Tom's Cabin (1852)

An antislavery account written by **abolitionist** and author Harriet Beecher Stowe and published as a novel in 1852. Many historians consider *Uncle Tom's Cabin* to be the most important antislavery work published in the United States.

With her book, Stowe introduced the brutal reality of slavery to many Americans. As a result, thousands embraced the abolitionist movement. The book's impact was so great that it is considered a cause of the Civil War (1861–1865). President Abraham Lincoln (1861–1865), who met Stowe in 1862, is reported to have said, "So this is the little lady who started this great war."

Harriet Beecher Stowe first wrote weekly installments of *Uncle Tom's Cabin, Or Life Among the Lowly,* for the abolitionist newspaper *The National Era* in 1851. The stories were written to protest the Fugitive Slave Act of 1850. This law required that all runaway slaves, regardless of where they were found, be returned to their owners. This meant that any former slave could be forced back into slavery. Stowe explained: "My heart was bursting with the anguish excited by the cruelty and injustice our nation was showing to the slave, and praying to God to let me do a little and cause my cry for them to be heard."

FROM NEWSPAPER TO BOOK

The response from readers of the weekly installments was immediate and enthusiastic. The following year, Stowe decided to publish *Uncle Tom's Cabin* in book form. It took time to find a publisher willing to print an antislavery novel, and only 10,000 copies of the first edition were printed. They sold out in a week. By the end of the year, 300,000 copies had been sold in the United States. The book was just as popular in Great Britain, selling about 200,000 copies in its first year. *Uncle Tom's Cabin* became one of the best-selling books of the nineteenth century. The French writer George Sand, a female novelist writing under a **pen name**, said of the book's popularity: "This book is in all hands and in all journals. It has, and will have, editions in every form; people devour it, they cover it with tears."

Uncle Tom's Cabin follows the story of Tom, an enslaved African American who is sold several times to different owners. Despite his brutal treatment throughout the book, Uncle Tom remains a forgiving character. This made him a hero for many readers. The cruel portrayal of the character Simon Legree, a Northerner who owned a plantation in Louisiana, instilled feelings of shame among many readers. Stowe used the experience of losing her own child to create the character of Eliza, a woman whose child is sold and taken away from her. Stowe was able to convince many readers that slavery was wrong by using real characters that they could identify with and feel sympathy for.

U–W

SOUTHERN ANGER

Most Southerners, however, were outraged by *Uncle Tom's Cabin* and claimed it was untrue. However, many of the characters were based on real people Stowe had met. Stowe had gotten the idea for the character of Uncle Tom from the autobiography of Josiah Henson. Henson had been born into slavery in Maryland, escaped to Canada in 1833, and published his autobiography in 1849.

In response to criticism, in 1853, Stowe published *A Key to Uncle Tom's Cabin: Presenting the Original Facts and Documents Upon Which The Story Is Founded*. Unlike *Uncle Tom's Cabin*, in which Stowe tried to be sympathetic to white Southerners as well as slaves, the new book was a much angrier attack on slavery.

Stowe had also intended her book to bring more Northerners to the cause of abolitionism. She felt that though most Northerners were not slave owners, they supported slavery by simply allowing it to exist. Stowe's powerful book had the desired effect.

HISTORY MAKERS
Harriet Beecher Stowe (1811–1896)

American author and abolitionist Stowe was born in 1811 in Litchfield, Connecticut. She was the seventh child of Lyman Beecher, a prominent preacher and abolitionist. Stowe first studied, and later taught at, the Hartford Female Seminary, which her older sister Catharine had founded. In 1832, Stowe moved to Cincinnati, Ohio, when her father became president of Lane Theological Seminary. There, her sister Catharine established the Western Female Institute, where Stowe continued to teach.

In Cincinnati, she met Calvin Stowe, a professor at Lane Theological Seminary. They were married in 1836 and had seven children. While there, Stowe witnessed slavery firsthand: Kentucky, a slave state, was just across the Ohio River. Stowe also talked with fugitive slaves, some of whom had escaped on the Underground Railroad. These experiences would influence the rest of her life.

In 1850, Calvin Stowe became a teacher at Bowdoin College in Maine. There, Harriet Beecher Stowe began writing *Uncle Tom's Cabin* as a response to the Fugitive Slave Law that had just been passed by Congress. After the book was published, Stowe became an international celebrity. She continued to write articles and books denouncing slavery.

For the rest of her life, Stowe was an outspoken supporter of African American rights. Stowe died on July 1, 1896, at the age of 85. She is buried next to her husband on the grounds of the Andover Theological Seminary in Massachusetts. Today, the house where Stowe lived for the last 23 years of her life is a museum open to the public.

By now, Northerners could no longer ignore the growing problem of slavery and its terrible consequences. Soon, the country would split over this issue, and the Civil War would begin.

See also: Fugitive Slave Law; Slave Narratives; Slavery; Underground Railroad.

FURTHER READING

Stowe, Harriet Beecher. Edited by Henry Louis Gates Jr. and Hollis Robbins. *The Annotated Uncle Tom's Cabin.* New York: W.W. Norton, 2006.

Underground Railroad

A system of safe houses and hiding places whose "stationmasters" and guides helped runaway slaves escape to freedom. The Underground Railroad was not a railroad at all but was named after the railroads that, at the time, were the fastest form of transportation.

The system also used railroad terms: the homes and businesses where runaway slaves could stop and rest were called "stations" and "depots." "Stations" were run by "stationmasters." The people who helped move fugitive slaves along the lines were called "conductors." Fugitive slaves were even sometimes referred to as "packages" or "freight" when stationmasters needed to talk in code.

Though many people, white and African American, participated in the Underground Railroad, it was not run by any single organization. Many people only knew about stops in their own towns or cities but did not realize that there were stops in other places. The Underground Railroad stretched for thousands of miles, from the slave states in the South to the free states in the Midwest. It also stretched south to north from Maryland, across Pennsylvania, into New York, and through New England. Yet, because of the secrecy necessary, it is almost impossible to trace the exact routes that runaway slaves took to reach free states. Thousands of slaves fled from the South each year before slavery was made illegal in 1865. It is estimated that around 1,000 African Americans per year were able to escape slavery during that time, many along the Underground Railroad.

BEGINNINGS

No one knows the exact date that the Underground Railroad started. Quakers, or members of the Religious Society of Friends, were the first group in the United States to speak out against slavery. Quakers began to help runaway slaves as early as the 1780s. During the same time, most Northern states had passed laws outlawing slavery. Because of this, free communities of African Americans in many Northern cities offered a safe place for escaping slaves.

However, the first Fugitive Slave Law of 1793, and later, the Fugitive Slave Law of 1850, permitted **slaveholders** to reclaim their runaway slaves, even if the slaves had moved to a free state. This meant that many African Americans had to leave the United States completely and seek freedom in Canada, where slaveholders could not legally reclaim them. As a result, the Underground Railroad

U–
W

HISTORY MAKERS

William Still: Father of the Underground Railroad

William Still (1821–1901) was born free in New Jersey. His father was a former slave who had purchased his own freedom. His mother, along with two of their children, had escaped from slavery in Maryland in 1807. To conceal their identities, they changed the family name from Steel to Still.

Still worked on his father's farm as a young boy. In 1844, at age 23, Still moved to Philadelphia, where he began working for the Pennsylvania Anti-Slavery Society, first as a janitor and mail clerk. Over time, his responsibilities increased, and when Philadelphia abolitionists organized a committee to help fugitive slaves, William Still was named its chairman. By the 1850s, Still had helped organize an extensive network of safe houses that became one of the most important Underground Railroad systems in the country. For his work, he became known as the Father of the Underground Railroad.

William Still kept detailed records of the committee's activities. In 1872, he published these records in a book called *The Underground Railroad.* The book also included the stories of hundreds of runaway slaves Still had interviewed in order to help friends and family find each other. During one interview, he discovered that one escaped slave was his own brother, Peter, who had been left behind when their mother escaped 40 years before. Unlike other accounts of the Underground Railroad that highlighted the bravery of white abolitionists, Still portrayed the slaves themselves as courageous people who had bravely achieved their freedom. William Still continued to fight for the rights of African Americans until his death in 1901.

stops in free states provided runaway slaves with safe places to hide on their way to Canada.

TRAVELING ON THE UNDERGROUND RAILROAD

The first step for any runaway slave was to escape from their slaveholder. Slaves usually had to do this for themselves, but sometimes a "conductor" would enter a plantation disguised as a slave to guide the runaways to freedom. Runaway slaves usually traveled alone or in small groups, so as not to draw attention to themselves. Night was the best time to travel, and many were guided north by simply heading in the direction of the North Star in the sky. Runaway slaves usually had to travel between 10 and 20 miles (16 and 32 km) to reach an Underground Railroad station, where they could stop to rest and eat. While they waited in a barn, a cellar, or another secret hiding place, a message would be sent to the next station to let the stationmaster know that runaways were on their way.

Conductors and stationmasters usually risked their lives and their property to help slaves reach safety. Many were threatened and attacked by slaveholders. Most conductors of the Underground Railroad were free African Americans or poor farmers, but some were wealthy whites, such as Quaker abolitionist merchant Thomas Garrett (1789–1871), whose home in Wilmington, Delaware, was an important stop on the Underground Railroad. One of the most famous conductors was Harriet Tubman (c. 1820–1913), who escaped from slavery in Maryland in 1849 and returned to the South about 20 more times to help guide more than 300 slaves to freedom. Some Southern whites helped fugitive slaves, but because their punishment would have been severe if they were discovered, details about them are not well known.

The Underground Railroad not only helped slaves escape, but some of its leaders–including free African American William Still–also organized a network to assist the runaways once they arrived. These vigilance committees, which were organized in large Northern cities such as New York, Philadelphia, and Boston, raised money and provided food and lodging for newly arrived African Americans. They also helped the freed slaves get settled in the committee and find work.

THE FUGITIVE SLAVE ACT

After the passage of the Fugitive Slave Law in 1850, activity on the Underground Railroad peaked. The new Fugitive Slave Law strengthened the original law of 1793 and made it legal for slaveholders to reclaim runaway slaves in free states. After the passage of the new Fugitive Slave Law, professional slave catchers were paid to travel into free states and reclaim runaway slaves for Southern slaveholders. The law gave slave catchers the ability to seize any African American suspected of having been a former slave, even if that person had been free his or her entire life. The Fugitive Slave Law outraged many Northerners and made even more people willing to assist escaping slaves.

STORIES OF THE UNDERGROUND RAILROAD

After slavery was abolished in 1865, the story of the Underground Railroad was kept alive by slave narratives written by former slaves, who told personal accounts of their escape. In addition, many former slaves were interviewed about their lives in a project funded by the federal government in the 1930s. However, most hiding places and secret passages, especially in cities, have either been damaged or hidden, because of new construction. There are some known stops on the Underground Railroad that are still preserved today, such as the secret attic in the Bialystoker Synagogue in New York City. However, because of the secrecy necessary to maintain Underground Railroad stops, many remain unknown.

See also: Bialystoker Synagogue; Canada and the Abolitionist Movement; Fugitive Slave Law; Garrett, Thomas;

Quakers; Slave Narratives; Tubman, Harriet.

FURTHER READING

Siebert, Wilbur H. *The Underground Railroad from Slavery to Freedom: A Comprehensive History.* Mineola, N.Y.: Dover Publications, 2007.

Still, William. *The Underground Railroad: Authentic Narratives and First-Hand Accounts.* Mineola, N.Y.: Dover Publications, 2007.

U.S. Mail, Censorship of

The suppression of **abolitionist** material sent through the U.S. mail. In the 1830s, many Southerners were directly confronted with the new abolitionist movement by way of the movement's literature sent through the mail. Although most Southerners were aware that an antislavery movement was building in the North, the abolitionist message had rarely affected them personally.

At this time, most abolitionist groups in the United States no longer supported the concept of gradualism, which called for a gradual end to slavery at some point in the future. Now, leaders of such groups as the American Anti-Slavery Society demanded immediatism, or the immediate end to slavery and the immediate establishment of civil rights for all African Americans. They sent out pamphlets and newspapers to spread the word and to persuade more Americans to join their cause.

In the summer of 1835, the American Anti-Slavery Society started a program that would increase the number of publications it produced so that their message could reach as many people as possible. The American Anti-Slavery Society was able to take advantage of recent advancements in printing that made it much cheaper to mass-produce material. In June, members began mailing thousands of antislavery publications to post offices in Northern and Southern states. They used city directories and other published lists to find the names and addresses of politicians, clergymen, and other local leaders to whom they could send the publications. The postal system also provided a safer way for the American Anti-Slavery Society to get their abolitionist message across, as it was often dangerous to send abolition agents and lecturers to the South.

THE CHARLESTON BREAK-IN

Reports of abolitionist literature arriving in Southern cities attracted little attention at first. On July 27, 1835, 30 copies of an abolitionist newspaper were discovered on a steamship arriving in Norfolk, Virginia. The *Norfolk Herald* reported the discovery, and word began to spread. Most people viewed the event as an isolated incident. However, an incident in Charleston, South Carolina, just two days later, brought the issue to national attention.

That day, July 29, 1835, a steamship arrived in Charleston with hundreds of abolitionist newspapers and journals published by the American Anti-Slavery Society. Many people angrily returned the publications to the post office once they saw what they were, and by the afternoon, others had heard what was in store for them. A **vigilance committee** called the South Carolina Association, made up of Charleston's most powerful citizens, confronted Postmaster Alfred Huger and demanded that he hand the publications over to them. Huger refused, but he agreed to hold them in his office until he received instructions from Postmaster General Amos Kendall. Yet just hours later, an angry mob of 200 to 300 men assembled at the post office and demanded that Huger hand over the abolitionist publications. A lieutenant of the City Guard was brought in to control the crowd, and they were ultimately sent away.

Later that night, another local vigilance society called the "Lynch Men" broke into the post office and stole the sack of abolition literature. The following evening, the Lynch Men publicly burned the papers in a large bonfire before a crowd of nearly 2,000 spectators.

THE SOUTHERN RESPONSE

Charleston postmaster Huger wrote to Postmaster General Kendall, asking for his help. He explained that only a "military force greater than the undivided population of Charleston" could have prevented the crowd from seizing the abolition papers. Huger admitted that he was not sure how much longer he could do his job and keep the mail safe from mobs. For the time being, Huger had arranged for a guard to escort the incoming mail safely from the Charleston steamboat landing to the post office. There, any abolitionist publications would be separated out of the mail and kept in the postmaster's office. Huger was not sure how long this could go on.

Even though it was illegal for postal workers to tamper with the mail in any way, Postmaster General Kendall supported Huger's decision to keep citizens from getting their hands on the abolitionist literature. Kendall wrote in a letter to Huger: "We owe an obligation to the laws, but a higher one to the community in which we live and, if the former be perverted to destroy the latter, it is patriotism to disregard them."

THE ABOLITIONIST DEFENSE

Abolitionists insisted that their publications were simply a way to spread their message to as many people as possible in order to bring about their ultimate goal: the end of slavery. However, many Southerners saw things differently. They accused the abolitionists of trying to start a slave rebellion by sending these publications into the South, where slaves could get their hands on them. During that summer, people in many different communities in the South were terribly frightened of a slave uprising. Planter Robert Gage of South Carolina described the atmosphere: "The daring and ingenious measures of the abolitionists begin to raise a storm in the south—the people are holding meetings in every section & expressing their determination to use every exertion to punish those who interfere with their property...."

Reaching out to white southerners Abolitionist groups denied that they were trying to start slave uprisings. They pointed out that they had only sent their publications to "respectable" white citizens, that slaves would never come across the publications, and that, even if they did, most slaves could not read. Yet Southerners insisted that abolitionist literature was a threat to public safety and, if unchecked, could bring about a complete breakdown of Southern society. In this way, Southerners were able to justify their support of the censorship of the mail.

Vigilance committees and violence By the middle of August 1835, communities all over the South had formed vigilance committees in preparation for the abolitionist material they expected to receive in the mail. Many Southern postmasters were instructed to separate out all the abolitionist publications from the mail. Then they either returned the newspapers and pamphlets to their publishers in the North, or they destroyed them. The vigilance committees were also directed to find and destroy any abolitionist newspapers or pamphlets that had accidentally gotten past the postmaster and entered the community. These committees had almost unlimited power in their towns and even set penalties for circulating antislavery literature that ranged from sending the offending individual out of the community to sentencing the individual to death.

LEGAL ACTION
President Andrew Jackson (1829–1837), a **slaveholder** himself, was angered by the abolitionist papers flooding into Southern post offices.

In response to Postmaster General Kendall's letter about the crisis, Jackson suggested that the abolitionist papers be delivered only to people who had subscribed to them and even those people should have their names taken down on record. By the fall of 1835, most states in the South had passed restrictions against circulating material that was considered a threat to public safety. Therefore, Southern postmasters were forced to uphold these state laws, which went against federal law that made censorship of the mail illegal. Most Southerners felt that protecting their safety was more important than following federal law.

Call for legislation President Jackson, in his annual message to Congress in December 1835, called for the passage of federal laws that would prohibit abolitionists from using the postal system to send their antislavery message to the South. However, in 1836, Congress ultimately concluded that the federal postal system could not legally censor the mail. Despite this, the Jackson administration continued to ignore the actions of Southern postmasters who destroyed antislavery publications sent by mail. This practice of censorship of the U.S. mail would continue in the South for the next 25 years.

Stronger anti-abolitionist views The American Anti-Slavery Society had hoped that by sending abolitionist materials through the mail to Southern communities, Northern abolitionists might enlist some moderate white Southerners to join their cause. Instead, it had the opposite effect. Most

Southerners had long believed that slavery should be treated as a local issue. They felt that Northerners had no right to attack something that was part of the Southern way of life and that the federal government had no reason to interfere with it either. The abolitionist postal campaign served to unite Southerners against a common enemy and made them even more determined to defend their right to practice slavery. Twenty-five years after a mob destroyed abolitionist publications in South Carolina, that state would become the first in the South to **secede** from the Union, thereby setting off the Civil War (1861–1865).

See also: American Anti-Slavery Society; Congress, United States; Gradualism; Immediatism.

Webster, Daniel (1782-1852)

Member of the U.S. Senate and House of Representatives (1813–1817 and 1823–1827) and secretary of state (1841–1843 and 1850–1852). Webster's impassioned pleas helped pass the Compromise of 1850, thus preserving the Union.

In 1822, Webster was elected a U.S. representative from Massachusetts, and four years later, he became a U.S. senator (1827–1841 and 1845–1850). President William Henry Harrison (1841) appointed Webster his secretary of state in 1840. When Harrison died a month after taking office, Webster stayed on as secretary of state under President John Tyler (1841–1845).

In 1845, Webster was reelected to the U.S. Senate. That same year, Texas entered the United States as a slave state. Soon after, the Mexican-American War (1846–1848) started because of the conflict over the southern border of Texas. As a result of the American victory in the war, the United States gained a huge **territory** from Mexico, which included present-day California, Nevada, Utah, and parts of Arizona, New Mexico, and Colorado. The already divided country had to decide if slavery should be allowed in the new territories.

Daniel Webster was opposed to slavery and did not want it to expand. However, he knew that banning slavery outright in these territories might cause Southern states to **secede** from the Union. This, he felt, was worse. Senator Henry Clay of Kentucky proposed a compromise that would allow California to enter the Union as a free state and other territories to decide for themselves whether to permit slavery. To appease the South, the compromise also included a Fugitive Slave Law requiring that escaped slaves anywhere in the country be returned to their owners.

Clay's proposal set off a debate in Congress that lasted eight months. In a powerful speech before the Senate on March 7, 1850, Daniel Webster urged Congress to support the compromise. He began his speech: "Mr. President, I wish to speak today not as a Massachusetts man, nor as a Northern man, but as an American . . . I speak today for the preservation of the Union. Hear me for my cause." Webster's speech, which lasted three-and-a-half hours, insisted

U–W

that "there can be no such thing as peaceable secession."

The following day, Webster's speech appeared in newspapers all over the country. He received high praise from many, but Northern **abolitionists** felt betrayed that he would consider such a compromise. In September, the Compromise of 1850 passed. Webster resigned from the Senate that year and became President Millard Fillmore's (1850–1853) secretary of state. Webster served until his death in 1852.

See also: Clay, Henry; Compromise of 1850; Fugitive Slave Law; Taylor, Zachary.

FURTHER READING

Harvey, Bonnie C. *Daniel Webster: Liberty and Union, Now and Forever.* Berkeley Heights, N.J.: Enslow, 2001.

Peterson, Merrill, D. *The Great Triumvirate: Webster, Clay, and Calhoun.* New York: Oxford University Press, 1988.

Remini, Robert V. *Daniel Webster: The Man and His Time.* New York: W.W. Norton & Company, 1978.

Women and the Abolitionist Movement

Women and their role in the American movement to end slavery. During the first two-thirds of the 1800s, thousands of women worked for the **abolitionist** cause. They wrote articles for abolitionist newspapers, gave speeches at abolitionist societies, and signed and delivered **petitions** to Congress calling for the end of slavery in the United States. Many also hosted antislavery fairs, in which they sold handmade clothing and quilts to raise money for the abolitionist cause. Many women were not only important leaders in the abolitionist movement but also eventual supporters of women's rights.

EXPERIENCES OF WOMEN IN THE MOVEMENT

Many American women were drawn to the antislavery cause because of strong religious or moral principles about the issue. Some women also sympathized with the plight of African Americans, because they, too, were denied many rights in American society. In 1837, abolitionist and women's rights activist Sarah Moore Grimke (1792–1873) wrote about the similarities between women and slaves: "Woman has no political existence. . . . She is only counted like the slaves of the South, to swell the number of law-makers who form the decrees for her government, with little reference to her benefit, except so far as her good may promote their own." Women who spoke publicly against slavery were often condemned and ridiculed. Many women began to realize that in order to have a real voice in the abolitionist movement they would need to fight for women's rights at the same time.

White women and African American women both participated in the abolitionist movement, though there were fewer black women for a number of reasons. Although all women in the United States had little freedom to participate in public life, African American women had even less freedom. After the passage of the Fugitive Slave Law in 1850, which made it possible for any African American to be sent into slavery if a **slaveholder** claimed he or she was an escaped slave, African American women were often in danger in public. Many white women abolitionists were either married to abolitionists or came from abolitionist families. However, those African American women who spoke out against slavery often used their own experiences to better illustrate the evils of slavery.

WOMEN ABOLITIONISTS

Angelina Grimke and Sarah Moore Grimke were the first women to speak publicly against slavery. As the daughters of a prominent South Carolina judge and **plantation** owner, the Grimke sisters had witnessed the brutality of slavery firsthand. They lectured about their experiences with slavery on their family plantation. Their outspoken views against slavery were condemned in the South, and eventually they moved to the North to spread the abolition message. In 1838, Angelina Grimke became the first woman ever to address a legal organization when she spoke to the Massachusetts State Legislature about abolitionism. Both sisters later became active in the women's rights movement, partly in response to the

Sojourner Truth, whose given name was Isabella Baumfree, was one of the most famous African American abolitionists and women's rights advocates. In 1826, after escaping from slavery in New York, she worked as a housekeeper in Massachusetts. In 1843, she joined the Methodist religion and began traveling and preaching about abolition.

attacks they received for speaking out against slavery.

Lucretia Mott (1793–1880) was also an important abolitionist and women's rights leader. Mott's family were members of the Society of

Friends, or Quakers. The Quakers were known for their antislavery work, leading Mott to become active in the abolitionist movement in Philadelphia. In 1833, Mott founded the Philadelphia Female Anti-Slavery Society. After the passage of the Fugitive Slave Law, her home became a stop on the Underground Railroad, a secret network of hiding places that helped runaway slaves escape to freedom. In the 1840s, Mott joined other women's rights leaders, including Susan B. Anthony (1820–1906) and Elizabeth Cady Stanton (1815-1902), to fight for the equal rights of both African Americans and women.

The two most famous African American women in the abolitionist movement were Harriet Tubman (1820-1913) and Sojourner Truth (1797-1883). Harriet Tubman had escaped from slavery in Maryland in 1849 and then secretly journeyed back to Maryland about 20 times, helping to free about 300 slaves. She was known for her bravery and determination. In her later years, Tubman also supported women's right to vote. In 1896, she served as a representative at the National Association of Colored Women's first annual convention.

Sojourner Truth escaped from slavery in 1826 and at the age of 46 became a traveling preacher, speaking out against slavery around the country. In 1851, Truth attended the Ohio Women's Rights Convention and gave one of the most famous women's rights speeches in American history. During her speech, Truth described her experiences both as a former slave and as a woman. Like many other women abolitionists, Truth had begun to realize that women's rights were also worth fighting for.

WOMEN IN ANTISLAVERY SOCIETIES

In 1833, abolitionist leader William Lloyd Garrison (1805-1879) helped found the American Anti-Slavery Society, which became the leading abolitionist society in the United States. It promoted the concept of immediatism, or the immediate end of slavery and the immediate establishment of equal rights for African Americans. At first, the society barred women from becoming members. Some male abolitionists simply believed that women should not participate in any political or moral cause. Some believed that women could do abolitionist work, but only behind the scenes, and that women should not become speakers for the American Anti-Slavery Society. Others felt that it was important to keep the issues of women's rights and abolitionism separate.

Importance of women However, some men recognized the benefits of having women join the abolitionist movement. Many abolitionist materials that were aimed at women appealed to their roles as wives and mothers in order to get them to sympathize with slave women who were often separated from their husbands and children. The most famous antislavery novel of the nineteenth century, *Uncle Tom's Cabin,* was written by abolitionist Harriet Beecher Stowe (1811-1896). Stowe purposely

History Speaks

Sojourner Truth Speaks at Women's Rights Convention

In May 1851, abolitionist Sojourner Truth attended the Women's Rights Convention in Akron, Ohio. At this meeting, many men, including ministers, spoke out against women's rights. They claimed that women were weak, and they voiced their beliefs that men were superior to women. Suddenly, Truth rose from her seat and asked Frances Gage, the president of the convention, if she could say a few words.

There is no formal record of Truth's speech. Newspapers wrote about it some weeks after the event took place. Then, in 1863, Frances Gage wrote her version of the event. Gage's account is the version that most people know today. Even though no one knows exactly what Truth said, it is clear that she made a huge impact at the convention and that her speech remains one of the most famous for women's rights.

Well, children, where there is so much racket there must be something out of kilter. I think that 'twixt the negroes of the South and the women at the North, all talking about rights, the white men will be in a fix pretty soon. But what's all this here talking about?

That man over there says that women need to be helped into carriages, and lifted over ditches, and to have the best place everywhere. Nobody ever helps me into carriages, or over mud-puddles, or gives me any best place! And ain't I a woman? Look at me! Look at my arm! I have ploughed and planted, and gathered into barns, and no man could head me! And ain't I a woman? I could work as much and eat as much as a man—when I could get it—and bear the lash as well! And ain't I a woman? I have borne thirteen children, and seen most all sold off to slavery, and when I cried out with my mother's grief, none but Jesus heard me! And ain't I a woman?

Then they talk about [intellect] . . . What's that got to do with women's rights or negroes' rights? If my cup won't hold but a pint, and yours holds a quart, wouldn't you be mean not to let me have my little half measure full. . . .

If the first woman God ever made was strong enough to turn the world upside down all alone, these women together ought to be able to turn it back, and get it right side up again! And now they is asking to do it, the men better let them.

Obliged to you for hearing me, and now old Sojourner ain't got nothing more to say.

U–W

appealed to her audience on an emotional level.

By 1839, the American Anti-Slavery Society had split into two groups. Some members found William Lloyd Garrison's beliefs to be too radical. One issue that many members disputed was Garrison's support of women's rights and the inclusion of women in the society. The leaders of the American Anti-Slavery Society that did not share Garrison's radical views broke away and formed the Liberty Party, a political party opposed to slavery. After 1840, women took on more active roles in the American Anti-Slavery Society. Maria Weston Chapman (1806–1885) worked closely with William Lloyd Garrison, helping to run the Boston office and edit *The Liberator*, Garrison's popular abolitionist newspaper. Other women, including Lucy Stone (1818–1893), Sojourner Truth, and Elizabeth Cady Stanton, served as traveling lecturers and organizers for local chapters of the American Anti-Slavery Society.

Strength through unity As the abolitionist and women's rights movements began to grow in the 1840s, many leaders felt that by working together they could strengthen both movements. In 1847, African American abolitionist Frederick Douglass (1818–1895) moved to Rochester, New York, to start an antislavery newspaper called the *North Star*. From lectures he had given there, Douglass knew that Rochester had an active abolitionist community that included many women. Through these women, Douglass met many promi-

nent women's rights leaders, including Susan B. Anthony, Lucretia Mott, and Elizabeth Cady Stanton. In 1866, Anthony, Stanton, and Douglass founded the American Equal Rights Association, which was established to protect the rights of all Americans.

THE WOMEN'S RIGHTS MOVEMENT
In 1840, the World Anti-Slavery Convention was held in London, attracting abolitionists from all over the globe, with the largest number coming from the United States. Elizabeth Cady Stanton and Lucretia Mott attended the convention with their husbands. However, women were not allowed to participate in any of the debates and had to sit behind a partition. Mott wrote in her diary that she was told "it would lower the dignity of the Convention and bring ridicule on the whole thing if ladies were admitted."

On to Seneca Falls As a result of their treatment at the convention, Stanton and Mott decided to hold a convention on women's rights. On July 19 and 20, 1848, they hosted the Seneca Falls Convention for women's rights in Seneca Falls, New York. This was the first women's rights convention in the United States. About 300 people, including 40 men, attended the convention. There, Stanton presented the "Declaration of Sentiments," a document modeled on the Declaration of Independence that called for equal rights for women in American society, including the right to vote. Sixty-eight women and 32 men signed the Declaration of Sentiments. Among the signers was Frederick Douglass.

A split in the movement In 1865, after the Thirteenth Amendment made slavery illegal in the United States, abolitionists continued to fight for the right for African Americans to vote. However, by 1869, the women's rights movement had split. Some leaders believed that the right to vote for all Americans was most important. These leaders, including Lucy Stone and Frederick Douglass, formed the American Woman's Suffrage Association. Other leaders, including Elizabeth Cady Stanton and Susan B. Anthony, believed their focus should only be on women's right to vote and formed the National Woman's Suffrage Association. In 1870, the Fifteenth Amendment gave African American men the right to vote. It was not until 50 years later that the Nineteenth Amendment gave women the right to vote.

See also: American Anti-Slavery Society; Douglass, Frederick; Garrison, William Lloyd; Immediatism; *North Star,* The; Quakers; Slave Narratives; Slavery; Truth, Sojourner; *Liberator The;* Tubman, Harriet; Underground Railroad.

FURTHER READING

Appleby, Joyce, ed. *Encyclopedia of Women in American History.* Armonk, NY: M.E. Sharpe, 2002.

Clinton, Catherine. *Harriet Tubman: The Road to Freedom.* Boston: Back Bay Books, 2005.

Kudlinski, Kathleen V. *Sojourner Truth.* New York: Aladdin Publishing, 2003.

Stowe, Harriet Beecher. Edited by Henry Louis Gates Jr. and Hollis Robbins. *The Annotated Uncle Tom's Cabin.* New York: W.W. Norton, 2006.

Truth, Sojourner. *The Narrative of Sojourner Truth.* New York: Cosimo Books, 2008.

U–
W

From a Letter to Representative John Holmes from Thomas Jefferson, April 22, 1820

In March 1820, Congress passed the Missouri Compromise, which allowed for two new states to be admitted to the Union, one free and one slave, and set a boundary for the extension of slavery into new Western **territories**. The following month, former president Thomas Jefferson (1801–1809) wrote to Massachusetts representative John Holmes about his concerns over this decision.

> I thank you, Dear Sir, for the copy you have been so kind as to send me of the letter to your constituents on the Missouri question. It is a perfect justification to them. I had for a long time ceased to read the newspapers or pay any attention to public affairs, confident they were in good hands, and content to be a passenger in our bark to the shore from which I am not distant. But this momentous question, like a fire bell in the night, awakened and filled me with terror. I considered it at once as the knell of the Union. It is hushed indeed for the moment. But this is a reprieve only, not a final sentence. A geographical line, coinciding with a marked principle, moral and political, once conceived and held up to the angry passions of men, will never be obliterated; and every new irritation will mark it deeper and deeper . . .

From Narrative of the Life of Frederick Douglass, an American Slave, Written by Himself, Frederick Douglass, 1845

Frederick Douglass escaped from slavery in 1838 and went on to become the most outspoken and respected African American **abolitionist** in the United States. In this excerpt from his autobiography, Douglass explains how he learned to read.

" Very soon after I went to live with Mr. and Mrs. Auld, she very kindly commenced to teach me the A, B, C. After I had learned this, she assisted me in learning to spell words of three or four letters. Just at this point of my progress, Mr. Auld found out what was going on, and at once forbade Mrs. Auld to instruct me further, telling her, among other things, that it was unlawful, as well as unsafe, to teach a slave to read. To use his own words, further, he said, "If you give a [slave] an inch, he will take an ell. Learning would ~spoil~ the best [slave] in the world. Now," said he, "if you teach that [slave] (speaking of myself) how to read, there would be no keeping him. It would forever unfit him to be a slave. He would at once become unmanageable, and of no value to his master. As to himself, it could do him no good, but a great deal of harm. It would make him discontented and unhappy." These words sank deep into my heart, stirred up sentiments within that lay slumbering, and called into existence an entirely new train of thought. It was a new and special revelation, explaining dark and mysterious things, with which my youthful understanding had struggled, but struggled in vain. I now understood what had been to me a most perplexing difficulty—to wit, the white man's power to enslave the black man. It was a grand achievement, and I prized it highly. From that moment, I understood the pathway from slavery to freedom. It was just what I wanted, and I got it at a time when I the least expected it. Whilst I was saddened by the thought of losing the aid of my kind mistress, I was gladdened by the invaluable instruction which, by the merest accident, I had gained from my master. Though conscious of the difficulty of learning without a teacher, I set out with high hope, and a fixed purpose, at whatever cost of trouble, to learn how to read. The very decided manner with which he spoke, and strove to impress his wife with the evil consequences of giving me instruction, served to convince me that he was deeply sensible of the truths he was uttering. It gave me the best assurance that I might rely with the utmost confidence on the results which, he said, would flow from teaching me to read. What he most dreaded, that I most desired. What he most loved, that I most

(continues)

(continued)

hated. That which to him was a great evil, to be carefully shunned, was to me a great good, to be diligently sought; and the argument which he so warmly urged, against my learning to read, only served to inspire me with a desire and determination to learn. In learning to read, I owe almost as much to the bitter opposition of my master, as to the kindly aid of my mistress. I acknowledge the benefit of both. . . .

The plan which I adopted, and the one by which I was most successful, was that of making friends of all the little white boys whom I met in the street. As many of these as I could, I converted into teachers. With their kindly aid, obtained at different times and in different places, I finally succeeded in learning to read. When I was sent of errands, I always took my book with me, and by going one part of my errand quickly, I found time to get a lesson before my return. I used also to carry bread with me, enough of which was always in the house, and to which I was always welcome; for I was much better off in this regard than many of the poor white children in our neighborhood. This bread I used to bestow upon the hungry little urchins, who, in return, would give me that more valuable bread of knowledge. . . .

From Uncle Tom's Cabin, Harriet Beecher Stowe, 1852

Many historians consider the novel *Uncle Tom's Cabin,* published in 1852, to be the most important American antislavery work. In this excerpt, slave-holder Tom Shelby explains to his wife that he must sell their slaves.

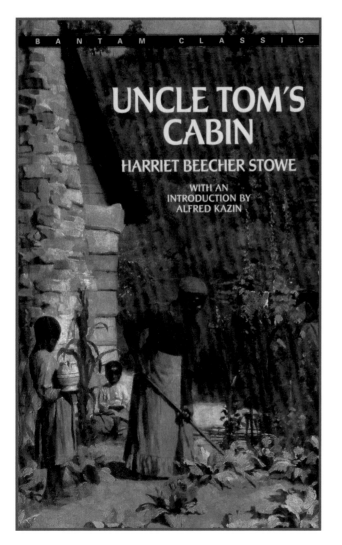

A cover from a mid-1900s edition of Harriet Beecher Stowe's *Uncle Tom's Cabin* shows the miserable work of enslaved plantation workers. Stowe's vivid story brought the daily difficulties of slaves to life and outraged Northern readers.

" Mr. and Mrs. Shelby had retired to their apartment for
the night. He was lounging in
a large easy-chair, looking over
some letters that had come
in the afternoon mail, and she was
standing before her mirror, brushing out the complicated braids and
curls in which Eliza had arranged her
hair . . . and turning to her husband,
she said, carelessly,

"By the by, Arthur, who was that
low-bred fellow that you lugged in
to our dinner-table to-day?"

"Haley is his name," said Shelby,
turning himself rather uneasily in his
chair, and continuing with his eyes
fixed on a letter.

"Haley! Who is he, and what may
be his business here, pray?"

"Well, he's a man that I
transacted some business with, last
time I was at Natchez," said Mr.
Shelby. . . .

"Is he a negro-trader?" said Mrs.
Shelby, noticing a certain embarrass-
ment in her husband's manner.

"Why, my dear, what put that into
your head?" said Shelby, looking up.

"Nothing, – only Eliza came in
here, after dinner, in a great worry,
crying and taking on, and said you
were talking with a trader, and that
she heard him make an offer for her
boy – the ridiculous little goose! . . . I
told Eliza," said Mrs. Shelby, as she
continued brushing her hair, "that
she was a little fool for her pains, and
that you never had anything to do
with that sort of persons. Of course,
I knew you never meant to sell any
of our people, – least of all, to such a
fellow."

"Well, Emily," said her husband,
"so I have always felt and said; but

the fact is that my business lies so
that I cannot get on without. I shall
have to sell some of my hands."

"To that creature? Impossible! Mr.
Shelby, you cannot be serious."

"I'm sorry to say that I am," said
Mr. Shelby. "I've agreed to sell
Tom."

"What! our Tom? – that good,
faithful creature! – been your faithful
servant from a boy! O, Mr. Shelby! –
and you have promised him his freedom, too, – you and I have spoken to
him a hundred times of it. Well, I can
believe anything now, – I can believe
now that you could sell little Harry,
poor Eliza's only child!" said Mrs.
Shelby, in a tone between grief and
indignation.

"Well, since you must know all, it
is so. I have agreed to sell Tom and
Harry both; and I don't know why I
am to be rated, as if I were a mon-
ster, for doing what every one does
every day."

"But why, of all others, choose
these?" said Mrs. Shelby. "Why sell
them, of all on the place, if you must
sell at all?"

"Because they will bring the highest sum of any, – that's why. I could
choose another, if you say so. The fellow made me a high bid on Eliza, if
that would suit you any better," said
Mr. Shelby.

"The wretch!" said Mrs. Shelby,
vehemently.

"Well, I didn't listen to it, a moment, – out of regard to your feelings, I wouldn't; – so give me some
credit."

"My dear," said Mrs. Shelby, recol-
lecting herself, "forgive me. I have
been hasty. I was surprised, and
entirely unprepared for this; – but

surely you will allow me to intercede for these poor creatures. Tom is a noble-hearted, faithful fellow, if he is black. I do believe, Mr. Shelby, that if he were put to it, he would lay down his life for you."

"I know it, – I dare say; – but what's the use of all this? . . ."

" . . . O, Mr. Shelby, I have tried . . . to do my duty to these poor, simple, dependent creatures. I have cared for them, instructed them, watched over them, and know all their little cares and joys, for years; and how can I ever hold up my head again among them, if, for the sake of a little paltry gain, we sell such a faithful, excellent, confiding creature as poor Tom, and tear from him in a moment all we have taught him to love and value? I have taught them the duties of the family, of parent and child, and husband and wife; and how can I bear to have this open acknowledgment that we care for no tie, no duty, no relation, however sacred, compared with money? I have talked with Eliza about her boy – her duty to him as a Christian mother, to watch over him, pray for him, and bring him up in a Christian way; and now what can I say, if you tear him away, and sell him, soul and body, to a profane, unprincipled man, just to save a little money? . . ."

"I'm sorry you feel so about it, – indeed I am," said Mr. Shelby; " . . . I didn't mean to tell you this Emily; but, in plain words, there is no choice between selling these two and selling everything. Either they must go, or *all* must. Haley has come into possession of a mortgage, which, if I don't clear off with him directly, will take everything before it. I've raked, and scraped, and borrowed, and all but begged, – and the price of these two was needed to make up the balance, and I had to give them up. . . . If you feel so to have them sold, would it be any better to have *all* sold?"

Mrs. Shelby stood like one stricken. . . . "This is God's curse on slavery! – a bitter, bitter, most ac-cursed thing! – a curse to the master and a curse to the slave! I was a fool to think I could make anything good out of such a deadly evil. . . ." 🙶

❗ *"House Divided" Speech, Abraham Lincoln, 1858*

In 1858, the Republican Party nominated former U.S. representative Abraham Lincoln to run against Stephen Douglas for his Senate seat in Illinois. Lincoln gave a now famous speech upon accepting the Republican nomination; the following is an excerpt.

> ❝ If we could first know where we are, and whither we are tending, we could better judge what to do, and how to do it. We are now far into the fifth year since a policy was initiated with the avowed object, and confident promise, of putting an end to slavery agitation. Under the operation of that policy, that agitation has not only not ceased, but has constantly augmented. In my opinion, it will not cease, until a crisis shall have been reached and passed. "A house divided against itself cannot stand." I believe this government cannot endure permanently half slave and half free. I do not expect the Union to be dissolved—I do not expect the house to fall—but I do expect it will cease to be divided. It will become all one thing, or all the other. Either the opponents of slavery will arrest the further spread of it, and place it where the public mind shall rest in the belief that it is in the course of ultimate extinction; or its advocates will push it forward, till it shall become alike lawful in all the States, old as well as new—North as well as South. . . . ❞

From Slave Narratives: Incident in the Life of a Slave Girl, Written by Herself, Harriet Jacobs, 1861

Harriet Jacobs's book was the first slave narrative written by a woman. The story told what it was like to be a female slave and described the hardships that were endured by enslaved women. In this excerpt, she describes her earliest memories.

“ I was born a slave; but I never knew it till six years of happy childhood had passed away. My father was a carpenter, and considered so intelligent and skilful in his trade, that, when buildings out of the common line were to be erected, he was sent for from long distances, to be head workman. On condition of paying his mistress two hundred dollars a year, and supporting himself, he was allowed to work at his trade, and manage his own affairs. His strongest wish was to purchase his children; but, though he several times offered his hard earnings for that purpose, he never succeeded. . . . [My parents] lived together in a comfortable home; and, though we were all slaves, I was so fondly shielded that I never dreamed I was a piece of merchandise, trusted to them for safe keeping, and liable to be demanded of them at any moment. . . . I had also a great treasure in my maternal grandmother, who was a remarkable woman in many respects. She was the daughter of a planter in South Carolina, who, at his death, left her mother and his three children free, with money to go to St. Augustine, where they had relatives. It was during the Revolutionary War; and they were captured on their passage, carried back, and sold to different purchasers . . . As [my grandmother] grew older she evinced so much intelligence, and was so faithful, that her master and mistress could not help seeing it was for their interest to take care of such a valuable piece of property. . . . She was much praised for her cooking; and her nice crackers became so famous in the neighborhood that many people were desirous of obtaining them. In consequence of numerous requests of this kind, she asked permission of her mistress to bake crackers at night, after all the household work was done; and she obtained leave to do it, provided she would clothe herself and her children from the profits. . . . **”**

✴ *The Emancipation Proclamation, 1863*

The Emancipation Proclamation was an order issued by President Abraham Lincoln (1861–1865) and signed on January 1, 1863, in the middle of the Civil War (1861–1865). It declared the end of slavery in all areas in rebellion against the Union.

❝ **By the President of the United States of America:**

A Proclamation.

Whereas, on the twenty-second day of September, in the year of our Lord one thousand eight hundred and sixty-two, a proclamation was issued by the President of the United States, containing, among other things, the following, to wit:

"That on the first day of January, in the year of our Lord one thousand eight hundred and sixty-three, all persons held as slaves within any State or designated part of a State, the people whereof shall then be in rebellion against the United States, shall be then, thenceforward, and forever free; and the Executive Government of the United States, including the military and naval authority thereof, will recognize and maintain the freedom of such persons, and will do no act or acts to repress such persons, or any of them, in any efforts they may make for their actual freedom.

"That the Executive will, on the first day of January aforesaid, by proclamation, designate the States and parts of States, if any, in which the people thereof, respectively, shall then be in rebellion against the United States; and the fact that any State, or the people thereof, shall on that day be, in good faith, represented in the Congress of the United States by members chosen thereto at elections wherein a majority of the qualified voters of such State shall have participated, shall, in the absence of strong countervailing testimony, be deemed conclusive evidence that such State, and the people thereof, are not then in rebellion against the United States."

Now, therefore I, Abraham Lincoln, President of the United States, by virtue of the power in me vested as Commander-in-Chief, of the Army and Navy of the United States in time of actual armed rebellion against the authority and government of the United States, and as a fit and necessary war measure for suppressing said rebellion, do, on this first day of January, in the year of our Lord one thousand eight hundred and sixty-three, and in accordance with my purpose so to do publicly proclaimed for the full period of one hundred days, from the day first above mentioned, order and designate as the States and parts of States wherein the people thereof respectively, are this day in rebellion against the United States, the following, to wit:

Arkansas, Texas, Louisiana, (except the Parishes of St. Bernard, Plaquemines, Jefferson, St. John, St. Charles, St. James Ascension, Assumption, Terrebonne, Lafourche, St. Mary, St. Martin, and Orleans, including the City of New Orleans) Mississippi, Alabama, Florida, Georgia, South Carolina, North Carolina, and Virginia, (except the forty-eight counties designated as West Virginia, and also the counties of Berkley, Accomac, Northampton, Elizabeth City, York, Princess Ann, and Norfolk, including the cities of Norfolk and Portsmouth[)], and which excepted parts, are for the present, left precisely as if this proclamation were not issued.

And by virtue of the power, and for the purpose aforesaid, I do order and declare that all persons held as slaves within said designated States, and parts of States, are, and henceforward shall be free; and that the Executive government of the United States, including the military and naval authorities thereof, will recognize and maintain the freedom of said persons.

And I hereby enjoin upon the people so declared to be free to abstain from all violence, unless in necessary self-defence; and I recommend to them that, in all cases when allowed, they labor faithfully for reasonable wages.

And I further declare and make known, that such persons of suitable condition, will be received into the armed service of the United States to garrison forts, positions, stations, and other places, and to man vessels of all sorts in said service.

And upon this act, sincerely believed to be an act of justice, warranted by the Constitution, upon military necessity, I invoke the considerate judgment of mankind, and the gracious favor of Almighty God.

In witness whereof, I have hereunto set my hand and caused the seal of the United States to be affixed.

Done at the City of Washington, this first day of January, in the year of our Lord one thousand eight hundred and sixty three, and of the Independence of the United States of America the eighty-seventh. **"**

Glossary of Key Terms

abolitionist A person opposed to slavery and in favor of ending it; in support of the antislavery viewpoint.

amend To change formally by modification, deletion, or addition.

amendment An alteration proposed or effected by the process of formally changing something, such as a constitution or other official document.

apprentice One bound to serve another for a prescribed number of years, usually to learn an art or trade.

armory A place where arms and military equipment are stored.

arsenal A collection of weapons.

bankrupt The condition of a debtor who, upon voluntary petition or one invoked by the debtor's creditors, is judged legally insolvent and unable to repay any debts.

bills Proposed laws.

border states During the American Civil War (1861–1865), the slave states of Missouri, Kentucky, Maryland, and Delaware that remained loyal to the Union. Later, in 1863, the slaveholding western counties of Virginia seceded from that state were admitted to the Union as the state of West Virginia.

British Parliament The legislative body of Great Britain, composed of the House of Commons and the House of Lords. The House of Commons is the democratically elected house of the Parliament, responsible for making laws and checking the work of Government; the House of Lords makes laws, provides a forum of independent expertise, and is the highest court in the land.

civil rights movement Beginning in the United States in the 1950s, the movement for racial equality that achieved national equal-rights legislation for African Americans.

colony A town or city established in a new land but controlled by a parent country.

colonists People who move from their homeland to settle a new town or city controlled by the parent country.

colonization An act or instance of establishing a settlement or colony.

comptroller A public official who audits government accounts and who sometimes certifies expenditures.

congregation The members of a specific religious group who regularly worship at a church or synagogue.

consecutive Following one after the other in order.

delegate A person authorized to act as representative for another; a deputy or an agent; a representative to a conference or convention.

discrimination Prejudiced or prejudicial outlook, action, or treatment.

emancipation The act or instance of freeing, as from slavery.

forgeries Illegal copies of a document.

Free-Soil Party Prior to the Civil War (1861–1865), a minor American political party that opposed the extension of slavery into U.S. territories and the admission of slave states into the United States.

fugitive A person who flees or tries to escape.

gag rule A rule instituted in Congress by Southern slaveholding states which stated that any petitions received by Congress that related to slavery would not be read or discussed in Congress; Congress ended the use of the gag rule in 1844.

immigrate To enter into and settle a region or country to which one is not native.

inaugural address A speech delivered at an inaugural, or formal swearing-in ceremony, especially by a United States president.

incumbent The holder of an office.

indentured servant A person who signs and is bound by documents to work for another for a specified time, especially in return for payment of travel expenses and maintenance.

insurrection An act or instance of revolting against civil authority or an established government.

Juneteenth Holiday commemorating June 19, 1865, when Union General Gordon Granger and his troops arrived in Galveston, Texas, and informed the slaves there of their freedom; still celebrated today as a national Independence Day for African Americans.

Know-Nothing Party Prior to the Civil War (1861–1865), a minor American political party whose members opposed immigration and naturalization, especially of Roman Catholic immigrants.

legislative Of or relating to the law.

libel A written statement that unjustly seeks to damage someone's reputation.

Louisiana Territory In 1803, a huge piece of land the United States purchased from France; the territory extended from the Mississippi River west to the Rocky Mountains.

Mexican Cession The huge territory—525,000 square miles (1.36 million square km)—acquired by the United States from Mexico after the Mexican-American War (1846–1848) under the terms of the Treaty of Guadalupe Hidalgo, which ended the war; the region included present-day California, Nevada, and Utah, as well as parts of Arizona, New Mexico, and Colorado.

migrate Moved from one habitat or country to another.

mutiny Open rebellion against authority, especially the rebellion of sailors against superior officers.

Nantucket An island off the southern coast of the state of Massachusetts and a part of that state.

narrative Something that is told or narrated; a story or personal account.

pacifist A person who subscribes to a belief of non-violence and who is opposed to war.

parallel Any of the imaginary lines encircling the earth's surface parallel to the plane of the equator and used to represent degrees of latitude north or south of the equator; in the study of abolitionism, the parallel 36'30° north of the equator was established by the 1820 Missouri Compromise as the line that separated free territory from territory where slavery would be permitted.

pen name An author's pseudonym, or false name, used on published works.

persecution The act or practice of harassing, especially those who differ in origin, religion, race, or social outlook.

petition A formal written application requesting a legal body, such as a legislature or a court, for a specific judicial action.

piracy Robbery committed at sea.

plantation A large agricultural estate, usually worked by resident labor; in the United States before the Civil War (1861–1865), most plantations were in the south and were worked by enslaved African Americans.

preliminary The first draft of a document or speech.

prostitution The work of a prostitute, one who sells sexual favors in return for money—often an enslaving and harsh life.

racist One who believes that his or her own race is superior to all others; holding discriminatory views or following prejudicial practices against a group based on the irrational belief that people with certain physical characteristics are inferior.

ratitied To officially confirm a treaty or other such document.

repeal To revoke or take back by law.

secede To withdraw from an organization.

segregation The condition of maintaining separate groups, especially the races.

slaveholder One who owns human beings in bondage as property.

suffrage The right to vote.

synagogue The house of worship of a Jewish congregation.

temperance Restraint from consuming alcohol or other intoxicating beverages.

territory A geographical area belonging to and under the jurisdiction of a governmental authority.

veto To refuse to approve.

vigilance committee A group of volunteers organized to suppress and punish crime summarily.

Whig Party An American political party formed about 1834 in opposition to Jacksonian Democrats and succeeded about 1854 by the Republican Party; associated chiefly with manufacturing, commercial, and financial interests.

Wilmot Proviso A proposed amendment to a $2 million appropriations bill intended for the final negotiations to resolve the Mexican-American War (1846–1848). The intent of the proviso, submitted by Democratic Congressman David Wilmot, was to prevent the introduction of slavery in any territory acquired from Mexico. The proviso did not pass in that session or in any other session when it was re-introduced over the course of the next several years.

Abolitionism 1830–1850. Available online. http://www.iath.virginia.edu/utc/abolitn/abhp.html

Altman, Linda Jacobs. *Slavery and Abolition in American History.* Berkeley Heights, N.J.: Enslow, 1999.

American Abolitionism. Available online. http://americanabolitionist.liberalarts.iupui.edu/

Appleby, Joyce, ed. *Encyclopedia of Women in American History.* New York: Book Builders LLC, 2002.

Bauer, K. Jack. *Zachary Taylor: Soldier, Planter, Statesman of the Old Southwest.* Baton Rouge: Louisiana State University Press, 1993.

Bergan, Michael. *The Lincoln-Douglas Debates.* Mankato, Minn.: Compass Point, 2006.

Berlin, Ira. *Many Thousands Gone: Two Centuries of Slavery in North America.* Cambridge, Mass.: Belknap Press, 2000.

Bernard, Catherine. *Sojourner Truth: Abolitionist and Women's Rights Activist.* (Historical American Biographies). Berkeley Heights, N.J.: Enslow, 2001.

Black History Month. Available Online. http://www.africanaonline.com/media.htm

Brackett, Virginia. *John Brown: Abolitionist.* New York: Chelsea House, 2001.

Burchard, Peter. *Frederick Douglass: For the Great Family of Man.* New York: Simon and Schuster, 2007.

Clinton, Catherine. *Harriet Tubman: The Road to Freedom.* Boston: Back Bay Books, 2005.

Currie, Stephen. *The Liberator: Voice of the Abolitionist Movement.* Words That Changed History Series. San Diego: Lucent Books, 2000.

Devillers, David. *The John Brown Slavery Revolt Trial: A Headline Court Case.* Headline Court Cases. Berkeley Heights, N.J.: Enslow Publishers, 2000.

Donald, David Herbert. *Charles Sumner and the Coming of the Civil War.* Naperville, Ill., Sourcebooks, 2009.

Douglass, Frederick. *The Narrative of the Life of Frederick Douglass, An American Slave, Written by Himself.* New York: Barnes and Nobles Classics, 2005.

Drew, Benjamin. *Refugees from Slavery: Autobiographies of Fugitive Slaves in Canada.* Pecos, N.Mex.: Dover Publications, 2004.

Eisenhower, John S.D. *Zachary Taylor.* New York: Times Books, 2006.

Etcheson, Nicole. *Bleeding Kansas: Contested Liberty in the Civil War Era.* Lawrence, Kan.: University of Kansas Press, 2006.

Equiano, Olaudah, and Vincent Carretta, eds. *The Interesting Narrative and Other Writings.* New York: Penguin Books, 2003.

Fauchald, Nick. *William Lloyd Garrison: Abolitionist and Journalist.* Mankato, Minn.: Compass Point, 2005.

Fehrenbacher, Don E. *The Dred Scott Case: Its Significance in American Law and Politics.* New York: Oxford University Press, 1997.

Fradin, Dennis Brindell. *Bound for the North Star: True Stories of Fugitive Slaves.* New York: Clarion Books, 2000.

Franklin, John Hope. *The Emancipation Proclamation.* Wheeling, Ill.: Harlan Davidson, 1995.

Friends of the Underground Railroad. Available Online. http://www.fourr.org/index.html

Griffith, Elisabeth. *In Her Own Right: The Life of Elizabeth Cady Stanton.* New York: Oxford University Press, 1984.

Grimke, Angelina Emily. *Walking by Faith: The Diary of Angelina Grimke, 1828–1835.* Columbia: University of South Carolina Press, 2003.

Guelzo, Allen C. *Lincoln and Douglas: The Debates That Defined America.* New York: Simon and Schuster, 2008.

Guelzo, Allen C. *Lincoln's Emancipation Proclamation: The End of Slavery in America.* New York: Simon and Schuster, 2004.

Harvey, Bonnie C. *Daniel Webster: Liberty and Union, Now and Forever.* Berkeley Heights, N.J.: Enslow, 2001.

Henson, Josiah. *The Life of Josiah Henson: Formerly a Slave, Now an Inhabitant of Canada.* Carlisle, Mass.: Applewood Books, 2002.

Hepburn, Sharon. *Crossing the Border: A Free Black Community in Canada.* Champaign: University of Illinois Press, 2007.

Horton, James Oliver, and Lois E. Horton. *Slavery and the Making of America.* New York: Oxford University Press, 2004.

Jacobs, Harriet. *Incidents in the Life of a Slave Girl.* Rockville, Md.: Arc Manor, 2008.

Jones, Howard. *Mutiny on the Amistad: The Saga of a Slave Revolt and Its Impact on American Abolition, Law, and Diplomacy.* New York: Oxford University Press, 1997.

Katz, William Loren. *The Westward Movement and Abolitionism 1815–1850.* A History of Multicultural America. Orlando, Fla.: Steck-Vaughn, 1993.

———. *Eyewitness: A Living Documentary of the African American Contribution to American History.* New York: Touchstone, 1995.

Marrin, Albert. *Commander in Chief: Abraham Lincoln and the Civil War.* New York: Dutton Juvenile, 2003.

May, Gary. *John Tyler.* New York: Times Books, 2008.

Mayer, Henry. *All on Fire: William Lloyd Garrison and the Abolition of Slavery.* New York: St. Martin's Press, 1998.

McArthur, Debra. *The Kansas-Nebraska Act and Bleeding Kansas in American History.* In American History. Berkeley Heights, N.J.: Enslow Publishers, 2003.

McCarthy, Timothy Patrick, and John Stauffer, eds. *Prophets of Protest: Reconsidering the History of American Abolitionism.* New York: New Press, 2006.

Mccomb, Marianne. *American Documents: The Emancipation Proclamation.* American Documents. Washington, D.C.: National Geographic Children's Books, 2005.

McGlowan, James A. *Station Master on the Underground Railroad: The Life and Letters of Thomas Garrett.* Jefferson, N.C.: McFarland and Company, 2004.

McGovern, George. *Abraham Lincoln.* New York: Times Books, 2009.

McPherson, James M. *Abraham Lincoln.* New York: Oxford University Press, 2009.

McNeese, Tim. *The Abolitionist Movement: Ending Slavery* (Reform Movements in American History). New York: Chelsea House, 2007.

Miller, William Lee. *Arguing About Slavery: John Quincy Adams and the Great Battle in the United States Congress.* New York: Vintage Books, 1998.

Morgan, Edmund S. *American Slavery, American Freedom.* New York: W.W. Norton, 2003.

Nagel, Paul C. *John Quincy Adams: A Public Life, a Private Life.* Cambridge, Mass.: Harvard University Press, 1999.

Neely, Jeremy. *The Border Between Them: Violence and Reconciliation on the Kansas-Missouri Line.* Columbia, Mo.: University of Missouri Press, 2007.

Newman, Richard S. *The Transformation of American Abolitionism: Fighting Slavery in the Early Republic.* Chapel

Hill: University of North Carolina Press, 2001.

Painter, Nell Irvin. *Sojourner Truth: A Life, a Symbol.* New York: W.W. Norton & Company, 1997.

Paulson, Timothy J. *Days of Sorrow, Years of Glory 1813–1850: From the Nat Turner Revolt to the Fugitive Slave Law.* Milestones in Black American History. New York: Jump at the Sun, 1994.

Peterson, Merrill, D. *The Great Triumvirate: Webster, Clay, and Calhoun.* New York: Oxford University Press, 1988.

Pierce, Alan. *The Lincoln-Douglas Debates.* Edina, Minn.: ABDO and Daughters, 2004.

Remini, Robert V. *Daniel Webster: The Man and His Time.* New York: W.W. Norton & Company, 1978.

———. *Henry Clay: Statesman for the Union.* New York: W.W. Norton & Company, 1993.

———. *John Quincy Adams.* New York: Times Books, 2002.

Reynolds, David S. *John Brown, Abolitionist.* New York: Alfred A. Knopf, 2005.

Scott, John A., and Robert Alan Scott. *John Brown of Harper's Ferry: With Contemporary Prints, Photographs, and Maps.* Makers of America. New York: Facts On File, 1993.

Schulman, Bruce J., ed. *Student's Guide to Congress.* Washington, D.C.: CQ Press, 2009.

Stauffer, John. *The Black Hearts of Men: Radical Abolitionists and the Transformation of Race.* Cambridge, Mass.: Belknap Press, 2004.

Sterling, Dorothy, ed. *We Are Your Sisters: Black Women in the Nineteenth Century.* New York: W.W. Norton, 1997.

Stowe, Harriet Beecher. Edited by Henry Louis Gates Jr. and Hollis Robbins. *The Annotated Uncle Tom's Cabin.* New York: W.W. Norton, 2006.

Tackach, James. *Abolitionist Movement.* American Social Movements. Farmington Hills, Mich.: Greenhaven Press, 2005.

The Terrible Transformation. Available online. http://www.pbs.org/wgbh/aia/home.html

Todras, Ellen H. *Angelina Grimke: Voice of Abolition.* North Haven, Conn.: Shoe String Press, Inc., 1999.

Wheelan, Joseph. *Mr. Adams's Last Crusade: John Quincy Adams's Extraordinary Post-Presidential Life in Congress.* New York: PublicAffairs, 2008.

White, Deborah Gray. *Let My People Go: African Americans 1804–1860.* The Young Oxford History of African Americans, vol. 4. New York: Oxford University Press, 1996.

White, Ronald C., Jr. A *Lincoln: A Biography.* New York: Random House, 2009.

Zeinert, Karen. *The Amistad Slave Revolt and American Abolition.* North Haven, Conn.: Shoe String Press, Inc., 1997.

———. *Tragic Prelude: Bleeding Kansas.* North Haven, Conn.: Shoe String Press, Inc., 2001.

Index

Page numbers in **boldface** indicate topics covered in depth in the A to Z section of the book.